Roses

Roses

Essential know-how and expert advice for gardening success

CONTENTS

This picture hints at the huge range of roses on offer, showing Climber, Ramblers, Ground Cover, and Shrub roses. There will usually be a selection that fits your garden perfectly.

UNDERSTANDING ROSES

Roses are among the most popular of all garden plants and have been enjoyed for thousands of years for their glorious flowers. A legacy of this long history is the diverse range now on offer, from huge ramblers that cascade over walls to tiny miniatures quite at home in containers. Some knowledge of the different rose types and their characteristics helps in choosing appropriate selections, ensuring that you get the best from these superb plants.

THE ALLURE OF ROSES

Roses are among the best-known and longest-cultivated of all flowers. They are revered and cherished around the world, and have deep cultural significance in numerous countries; in some they have even been adopted as national emblems. The enduring popularity of roses is partly due to their associations with love, which stems from their beautiful appearance and, often, scent. However, they are also loved by gardeners for their utility: many are tolerant, disease resistant, and have extended flowering seasons thanks to their continual improvement by breeders.

Roses are loved around the world for their beauty and fragrance.

FLOWERS OF ROMANCE

Roses have long been symbols of romance and fervor; the Romans recounted legends linking red roses to Aphrodite, goddess of love, while early Christians came to associate the rose with the Virgin Mary's virtue. Between 1455 and 1487, the flower was used as a symbol for both sides in the contest for control of the English throne—the Wars of the Roses. By the end of the 17th century, roses were highly prized in the gardens of European nobility. New selections were developed by growers, a trend which intensified as the range grown in the West was enriched by new arrivals from the Far East. Rose-growing attracted prominent and influential enthusiasts, such as Empress Joséphine, consort of French emperor Napoleon, who sought to grow every kind of rose in her garden at Malmaison in Paris.

In the late 19th century, roses—many of which had been raised in France—became the flower of choice in society, with some, such as Tea roses and Noisettes, kept under glass for cutting.

By 1837, British grower Thomas Rivers had 100,000 roses at his nursery to meet demand from landowners who maintained formal rose gardens. However, by the end of the 19th century, roses began to be grown more casually in various forms and in mixed plantings.

For today's growers, the historic symbolism of roses is overlaid with the romance of the golden age of gardening, when old roses cascaded in abandon from pergolas and trellises in cottage gardens and the walls of now-lost country estates.

Rosa gallica var. *officinalis* was the emblem of the English House of Lancaster.

Elegant *Rosa* 'Maréchal Niel' was grown under glass by the Victorians.

Roses became popular for mixed plantings outdoors in the 20th century.

ESSENTIAL GARDEN PLANTS

Roses are versatile plants that have a place in almost any garden. Shrub roses may be the most familiar type of rose, but others can be grown successfully in containers, and Ramblers can cover entire outbuildings. Roses are quite easy to grow and most have a long flowering season, making them great value. Continual improvement by breeders has kept these plants relevant, with new cultivars resistant to disease and tolerant of more varied climatic conditions. New selections that are attractive to pollinators have also seen roses reappraised for wildlife benefits.

Species roses such as *R. sweginzowii* have single flowers that attract bees.

A bunch of red roses is the classic Valentine's Day love token.

Miniature roses are often grown as potted plants for display indoors.

THE ROSE INDUSTRY

There are around 300 species of rose, but just a few of these have given rise to the thousands of cultivars grown around the world. Their adaptability to a wide range of climates and variety in appearance and scent have helped to make roses among the most loved plants by gardeners and florists. Rose flowers are available in almost any imaginable color, making them suitable for all occasions—from Valentine's Day tokens of love to weddings and funerals. Today, roses for the cut flower market are often raised in tropical climates and exported around the world. Their cultivation is a big business, with an estimated global value in excess of $10 billion in 2022.

SCENT FROM HEAVEN

If asked to choose a garden plant with good scent, many people would select a rose. The flowers have become synonymous with perfume, even though not all have a fragrance. The perfume of roses is complex and varies considerably from rose to rose, and even one flower will vary in its scent as the bloom ages.

Some old roses have a rather fruity scent, others sweet and fresh, while a few smell almost creamy. Then there are roses with musk fragrance—a rather distinctive scent that carries well on the air. Most renowned of these are *R. moschata* and the Ramblers derived from it, such as 'The Garland'. Some roses smell of myrrh (similar to cough drops or aniseed). Tea roses have flowers with a distinct, herbal but sophisticated smell of tea leaves. Modern cultivars, many of which have a strong, fruity scent, have become the most popular fragrant garden roses.

Rose fragrance varies greatly between cultivars; not all are scented.

A rose tunnel makes a spectacular garden feature. It can be covered with climbers that repeat through the summer or with quick-growing ramblers.

ROSES FOR TODAY'S GARDENS

Although roses are among the oldest of garden plants, they are generally tough, adaptable, and well-suited to the rigors of modern life. Today's cultivars are easy to grow and many will flower for months, producing blooms in a range of sizes, shapes, and hues. There is a rose for almost every place in the garden and for every kind of garden, whether large or small, formal or inspired by the wild.

Some modern roses will thrive in pots, making them well-suited to small paved spaces.

EASY TO GROW

Roses have a reputation for being hard to grow. This was largely founded on gardeners' experiences with early hybrids, which breeders produced for their beauty, but often at the expense of resistance to disease and the elements. The roses available today—notably modern Shrub roses, Climbers, Hybrid Tea, and Floribunda types—are far more resilient, needing little attention once they are established. Some, such as Ground Cover roses, Species roses, and Ramblers, perform to a standard that few other plants can equal, surviving with virtually no care after planting.

Growing modern roses is extremely easy, not least because the forgiving nature of these plants means that you can learn as you go. Simple pruning, feeding once a year, and deadheading (the removal of faded blooms) are often the only tasks you need to carry out as long as you choose the right plants for the right locations (see pp.26–27).

When planting, choose a rose suited to the location (see p.26–27). This will give your plant the best chance from the start.

GOOD FOR WILDLIFE

Planting roses can help make your garden attractive to insects, birds, and other wildlife.

- Choose roses that have single or semi-double flowers, rather than a dense mass of petals, to attract bees and other pollinators.
- Allow some flowers to develop into hips; these are a source of winter food for birds.
- Choose species or cultivars that are resistant to diseases, such as blackspot (see p.44), to avoid having to spray with fungicide.
- Aphids love roses; rather than spraying, let insects such as ladybugs and hoverflies control the aphid populations.

Rose hips attract birds and mammals to your garden in winter.

MONTHS OF INTEREST

Unlike many garden plants that bloom only for a couple of weeks, some roses can flower for nine months of the year or even longer. Plants such as *R. banksiae* 'Lutea' and *R. xanthina* 'Canary Bird' reliably flower once in early spring, bringing welcome color into the garden, while modern Shrub roses, Climbers, Hybrid Tea, and Floribunda roses may repeat flower through summer and into fall as long as they are regularly deadheaded; the most prolific will flower until the first air frosts. Some cultivars, such as *R. rugosa* 'Alba', produce attractive hips in fall and winter, while *R. sericea* subsp. *omeiensis* f. *pteracantha* is remarkable all winter for its ornamental thorns.

Even a dusting of snow will not stop some roses flowering.

Regular deadheading promotes the formation of more blooms, keeping roses that repeat flower colorful through summer.

WIDE VARIETY

There is a rose to suit every taste and every style of garden. Formal sites suit rose gardens with plantings of neat, upright roses, such as Floribunda and Hybrid Tea roses that flower for months. Old Garden roses and Climbers are best suited to more relaxed cottage and country gardens, while even the smallest garden can be a home to a Patio or Polyantha rose in a pot.

Flower forms are equally diverse, ranging from large, lush double blooms to classic high-centered flowers that are perfect for cutting. You may prefer the simpler charms of wild or China roses or the loosely formed blooms of Tea roses. Color-wise, take your pick—almost every hue is available, even purple and blue.

Rosa **Blue Moon** (**'Tannacht'**) is the best-known blue-tinted rose.

HARDY AND TOUGH

When it comes to plants, don't confuse beauty with frailty. Roses are surprisingly tough and able to tolerate a wide range of conditions. Once established, roses can stand summer drought and are among the few garden plants that can thrive in hot—even tropical—conditions, as well as in continental climates with their bitterly cold winters. If affected by an exceptionally dry summer they usually bounce back quickly the following year.

Roses seldom need additional watering once established, although some older, more delicate kinds may benefit from watering in prolonged dry spells. Conversely, many modern roses have been developed to tolerate wet weather, which can destroy blooms of more delicate types if it strikes at flowering time. If you live in a rainy area, it is advisable to avoid double-flowered Old Garden roses with delicate petals.

Few roses flower very early in the year, so they do not often run the risk of frost damage, but it is sensible to grow spring-flowering varieties against a protective house wall. Less hardy types include some Tea and China roses, which are rather uncommon in today's gardens.

HOW GARDEN ROSES DEVELOPED

Roses have been enjoyed by diverse cultures for millennia and have a fascinating history. Over centuries, growers have selected roses for characteristics such as flower form and color, scent, or repeat flowering, creating distinct races that are evocative of the era in which they were raised. Today's breeders have selected qualities such as weather and disease resistance to make roses ideal for modern gardens.

The vast range of roses now available is the result of many centuries of careful breeding and selection.

EARLY CULTIVATED ROSES

Wild roses grow naturally throughout the northern hemisphere, in Europe, North America, the Middle East, and Asia; none originate from south of the equator. Roses are thought to have first been cultivated in China thousands of years ago for the beauty of their flowers or their edible hips, and later records show that they were grown by the Romans and peoples in the Middle East.

By the 12th century, Gallica roses including *Rosa gallica* var. *officinalis* and *R. gallica* 'Versicolor' had begun to be cultivated in Northern Europe, followed by Damask, Alba, and then Centifolia roses, the first of which appeared at the end of the 16th century, probably from crosses made by the Dutch between Damask and Alba roses.

China roses arrived from the East in the late 18th century and may have been used in the development of Portland roses by breeders in France. Tea roses, initially also from the Far East, arrived in the early 19th century, the pale pink 'Hume's Blush' being among the first.

French breeders were responsible for many more rose types, including Bourbon roses, Hybrid Perpetuals, and Noisettes (although the first of these came from the US).

The first Hybrid Tea rose, pink *R.* 'La France', was developed in 1867 by breeding Hybrid Perpetual roses with Tea roses to generate elegant yet robust and—importantly—repeat-flowering plants. The range expanded with yellow selections before the turn of the century, an era when Hybrid Teas would dominate in gardens around the world.

The flowers of *Rosa gallica* 'Versicolor' have been enjoyed for centuries.

Tea rose 'Climbing Devoniensis' was raised in the early 19th century.

Elegant silver-pink *Rosa* 'La France' was the first true Hybrid Tea rose.

Hybrid Musk roses, such as 'Penelope', were developed by clergyman and rosarian Joseph Pemberton.

Rose breeding continues to this day; many thousands of crosses are made to create a first-rate new selection.

ROSES INTO THE 20TH CENTURY

In the first decades of the new century, UK clergyman and casual rose breeder Joseph Pemberton developed Hybrid Musk roses—plants such as 'Penelope' and 'Cornelia' that had clusters of medium-size flowers. His legacy was enriched after his death by one of his gardeners, J. A. Bentall. We have Danish nurseryman Dines Poulsen to thank for Floribunda roses, development of which involved Polyantha roses to provide a multi-flowered habit; the first true examples appeared in the 1930s.

Floribundas and Hybrid Tea roses came to define rose breeding in the 20th century. Repeat-flowering Climbers, many derived from Hybrid Tea roses, became popular as the rise in suburban gardens created a new need to cover ugly fences, while ever-smaller plots drove interest in Miniature roses (which had been grown as potted plants at least a century earlier). These in turn gave way to larger, sturdier Patio roses that were suitable for growing in containers. By the final decades of the century, disease resistance was the key requirement for any new rose, as environmental concerns saw the withdrawal of many pesticides.

The healthy growth and distinctive blooms of *Rosa* FOR YOUR EYES ONLY ('Cheweyesup') result from the work of innovative breeders.

ROSES TODAY

Today's breeders are producing plants that need less care than ever. There have been big improvements among Ground Cover and Patio roses, Climbers and even Ramblers, some of which now repeat flower and need less pruning. Plants known as English Roses, first developed by rosarian David Austin, are popular, combining the grace, flower form, and fragrance of Old Garden roses with the latest standards of vigor, repeat flowering, and disease resistance.

Roses with open-centered flowers are more often seen, reflecting a move to wildlife-friendly gardens. The thirst for new colors and patterns continues; for example, UK grower Chris Warner used *Rosa persica* to produce selections such as FOR YOUR EYES ONLY ('Cheweyesup'), which has distinctive dark-eyed blooms.

CLASSIFYING ROSES

Over the centuries that roses have been cultivated in gardens around the world, numerous distinct types have been developed. Their diversity in form has been classified in various ways, giving rise to exotic names such as Damask, Noisette, and Bourbon. The UK's Royal Horticultural Society recognizes 27 different types, while the American Rose Society has three main classes, within which are many divisions. For simplicity, however, roses that have roughly similar characteristics and growing requirements can be placed informally into the five groups described below.

GROUP 1: MODERN GARDEN BUSH ROSES

This group includes the most widely grown rose types; many are recent introductions, bred to suit today's gardens. These roses are bushy and usually repeat bloom. They thrive in dedicated rose gardens and some work well in mixed plantings. There are thousands of cultivars with more launched each year. This large group includes the following types.

HYBRID TEA ROSES Also known as Large-Flowered Bush roses, these are the best-known of all roses. Upright-growing, they reflower in flushes all season, their large flowers carried singly or in small groups atop stems.

FLORIBUNDA ROSES Also called Cluster-Flowered Bush roses, these somewhat stiff, upright plants produce large clusters of medium-size flowers consistently through summer and fall, creating a mass of color.

SHRUB ROSES These roses are variable, but most are bushy, spreading plants that integrate well into mixed plantings. Not all repeat flower. Breeding in recent decades includes David Austin's popular English roses (see p.15).

GARNETTE ROSES Developed in Germany in the 1940s for the flower trade, these are seldom grown in gardens.

Hybrid Tea rose, *Rosa* POETRY IN MOTION ('Harelan').

Floribunda rose, *Rosa* FERDY ('Keitoli') produces dense clusters of color.

Shrub rose, *Rosa* DESDEMONA ('Auskindling') repeat flowers well.

Patio rose, *Rosa* 'Ballerina'.

GROUP 2: SMALL BUSH ROSES

Most of these small roses were developed in recent decades and make great container plants. They are repeat flowering but have little scent.

PATIO ROSES This is a new group of plants that have a compact habit and bear small flowers.

POLYANTHA ROSES The earliest of these roses date back to the 19th century. Most form small plants with clustered, small, double flowers.

MINIATURE ROSES The smallest of roses, these are often grown in pots indoors, in window boxes, or used as bedding.

GROUP 3:
OLD GARDEN ROSES

The group is extremely diverse, its members having varying growth habits.

GALLICA ROSES These dense, suckering bushes produce clusters of richly colored, scented flowers just once in the summer.

SPECIES ROSES Also called wild roses, they are usually large, arching shrubs with single flowers, produced in summer.

ALBA ROSES These are large, leafy plants bearing clusters of pastel-colored, scented flowers just once in summer.

CENTIFOLIA ROSES These have tall, spiny stems bearing blowsy, scented double flowers once in summer.

DAMASK ROSES These old roses are grown for their clusters of scented, open-centered flowers, which are usually produced once in summer.

DAMASK PORTLAND ROSES Compact and dense, these shrubs reflower well, usually with fully double blooms.

MOSS ROSES Rather tall and "stemmy" with mosslike growth on buds, these roses are usually double-flowered.

BOURBON ROSES Typically vigorous and repeat-flowering, these roses have scented blooms in small clusters. Some climb.

HYBRID PERPETUAL ROSES Vigorous and often tall, many repeat flower with trusses of (usually) scented large double blooms.

HYBRID MUSK ROSES These vigorous roses have arching stems bearing trusses of scented, usually double, flowers.

CHINA ROSES Well-branched with slender stems, these sometimes tender roses bear single or double flowers.

RUBIGINOSA ROSES These rambling, arching shrubs flower freely once a year.

RUGOSA ROSES Sturdy, suckering plants, these are single- or double-flowered, often repeating well.

SPINOSISSIMA ROSES These shrubby, suckering, prickly plants have delicate foliage; they flower once in summer.

TEA ROSES The loose, double blooms of these roses have a spicy scent. Repeat-flowering, they may be shrubs or climbers.

Gallica rose, *Rosa* 'Cardinal de Richelieu' has dark purple, double flowers.

Centifolia rose, *Rosa* 'Fantin Latour' shows off its sumptuous flowers.

Moss rose, *Rosa* 'William Lobb' has distinctive mossy growth on its buds.

Hybrid Musk rose, *Rosa* 'Felicia' has fully double blooms.

Wild Spinosissima rose, *Rosa* 'Stanwell Perpetual'.

Tea rose, *Rosa* 'Climbing Lady Hillingdon' has a spicy scent.

Noisette rose, Rose 'Madame Alfred Carrière'.

Rambler rose, Rosa 'Alister Stella Gray', has rosette-shaped blooms.

GROUP 4: CLIMBING ROSES AND RAMBLERS

This highly diverse group brings together roses that need some type of support. Note that this is also a requirement of some roses not included in this group, such as some Bourbon and Polyantha roses. Breeders have also produced climbing versions of Floribunda and Hybrid Tea roses.

BOURSAULT ROSES These rather obscure climbers were raised in France in the 19th century. They are vigorous, thornless, and flower once early in the season.

CLIMBERS This itself is a diverse class. Its members tend to have large flowers held singly or in clusters; most respond well to deadheading, repeating well into fall.

NOISETTE ROSES These plants are usually climbers that produce showy clusters of flowers. They repeat flower through the season from midsummer, and usually have a Tea rose–like scent. Some are rather tender.

RAMBLERS These vigorous plants have long, flexible, and often rather thorny stems. Most members of the group flower only once per season. The clustered flowers are fairly small but profuse and may be followed by hips.

NAMING ROSES

The nomenclature of roses can be confusing. All roses belong to the genus Rosa, in which there are several hundred species. Those produced by plant breeders have a cultivar (short for "cultivated variety") name, which is recognized by horticulturalists worldwide. This may refer to the breeder's name (for example Rosa 'Ausbord', produced by UK breeder David Austin) or an almost impenetrable string of characters (for example, Rosa 'Tan96138'). It is always set in Roman, not italic, type surrounded by single quotation marks. Roses may also be known by their trade designation which is given by the nursery trade to make the name more appealing to the public in a particular country (because breeders may just register a number or name in a foreign language).

For example, Rosa 'Ausbord' is sold and is best known as GERTRUDE JEKYLL. Trade names have no quotation marks and are by convention set in a distinctive typeface. Note that one rose can be sold under different trade names in different countries.

GROUP 5: GROUND COVER ROSES

Members of this group are all low-growing or spreading plants that can form effective cover. Some are shrubby and branched, others lower, growing like unsupported ramblers, with long, often unbranched stems snaking across the ground, rooting as they go. They may repeat or be once-flowering, producing profuse, small, single or double blooms.

Ground Cover rose Rosa 'Chewharla' displays its multicolored flowers.

Rosa 'Ausbord' is widely sold and best known as GERTRUDE JEKYLL.

ROSE FLOWER SHAPES

Across the thousands of rose cultivars there are eight basic flower forms—the shape that flowers have at their peak (flower form changes with age, blooms becoming more cupped and open-centered with maturity.

Rose flowers may be single (normally with five but up to seven petals), semi-double (around 16 petals, with stamens showing), double (17–30 petals) or fully double (more than 30).

Most wild roses have **flat** flowers, single blooms with overlapping or spaced petals. This form is also found in groups of cultivated roses, including China roses, Rugosa roses, Climbers, Ramblers, and Hybrid Tea roses. Some semi-double roses also develop a flat form; all are open-centered, which allows good access for pollinating insects. **Cupped** flowers are similarly open-centered and good for pollinators. This flower form is typical of many semi-double blooms and found in most classifications.

Pointed or high-centered blooms are associated with semi-double to fully double Hybrid Tea roses and some tea roses. The central petals are tightly packed while outer ones fall open. The best-known flower form is probably **urn-shaped**; this is seen among semi-double to fully double Hybrid Tea roses but also climbers and some patio and miniature roses. **Rounded** flowers are similar but more cupped and are common among double and fully double Floribunda roses.

Many Old Garden roses and Shrub roses have **rosette** form flowers, in which the double or fully double blooms are flattish and unstructured, with their petals overlapping. This appearance is taken a stage further with the **quartered rosette** flower form, where blooms develop an almost cruciform (cross-shaped) petal arrangement. The most densely packed of all petals are in the **pompom** flower form. These are small, rounded flowers featuring masses of small petals.

Flat flowers are displayed by this Group 3 Species rose, *Rosa xanthina* 'Canary Bird'.

Cupped flowers are seen on the Group 4 Climber OPEN ARMS ('Chewpixcel').

Pointed flowers are seen on the Group 1 Hybrid Tea rose 'National Trust'.

Urn-shaped flowers of Group 1 Hybrid Tea rose PEACE ('Madame A. Meilland').

Rounded flowers are seen on Group 1 Floribunda rose AMBER QUEEN ('Harroony').

Rosette flowers are displayed by Group 3 Gallica rose 'Charles de Mills'.

Quartered rosette flowers from Group 1 Shrub rose WILLIAM SHAKESPEARE 2000 ('Ausromeo').

Pompom flowers are produced by Group 4 Rambler *Rosa* 'Félicité-Perpétue'.

This bushy *Rosa* Absolutely Fabulous ('Wekvossutono') is a healthy example of a modern Floribunda rose.

HOW ROSES GROW

To understand how to get the best from your roses it helps to appreciate how they grow and the characters that they will develop when mature. Most roses on the market today are bud-grafted—raised in a way that makes them strong-growing and reliable, despite producing the odd sucker. Roses have quite varied growth habits, either naturally or as a result of how they are cultivated, in some cases producing stems that require support.

Some rose species are raised from seed or suckers; they are not grafted but grow on their own roots.

BUD-GRAFTED ROSES

Most roses you can buy at a garden center or nursery have been produced by grafting together two different plants. One plant is chosen for its desirable flowers and foliage, while the other is from a different species or cultivar that is known for its strong growth and resistance to disease. The result has the best qualities of both plants.

Grafting is carried out in winter, when plants are dormant. A bud-bearing section of stem from one plant (called the scion)—is spliced into the stem of another (the rootstock) that will provide the roots of the resulting graft. The bud grows, forming a living union (the knobbly bit visible just above the roots), and goes on to produce a shoot that will develop into the above-ground parts. This technique—known as bud-grafting—requires considerable skill; professional growers use it to produce plants that quickly develop into vigorous, sale-size roses with strong root systems. The main downside of growing bud-grafted roses is that the rootstock may produce suckers (see *p.35*) that will need to be removed.

Roses grown on their own roots can also be found for sale. These are usually rose species, or those that form a suckering bush that is easily divided from its parent plant.

The vast majority of roses sold at garden centers are grafted plants.

TOP TIP PLANT YOUR ROSES WITH THE GRAFT UNION JUST BELOW SOIL LEVEL. THIS WILL HELP DISCOURAGE UNWANTED SUCKERS ARISING FROM THE ROOTSTOCK AND SHOULD MEAN THAT THE PLANT IS FIRM IN THE GROUND—AN IMPORTANT CONSIDERATION FOR EXPOSED SITES.

Firm graft union just below soil surface ....

Well-branched, healthy root system

A healthy rose will have strong roots, a well-established graft union, and ideally at least three strong, well-placed stems.

DEALING WITH TALLER ROSES

Some roses, most notably Centifolia and Moss roses, develop tall, arching stems that need support, especially when the plants are covered in heavy blooms. You can provide the necessary support by tying stems to tree stakes or to tripods made of wooden poles; also try looping a wire hoop around a group of stems so they keep each other vertical. Even taller roses such as Bourbon and Hybrid Perpetuals can be controlled using an old technique called pegging down, whereby stems are carefully bent and fastened to the ground. From these develop side shoots that form an arching mound of flowers.

Taller-growing Shrub roses may need some support from low stakes as their stems are slender and top growth heavy.

Very tall roses, such as some Hybrid Perpetuals may be pegged down to form an impressive mound of flowers.

Roses trained as standards should always be staked for support.

STANDARD ROSES

Standard roses carry their leaf and flower growth on top of a tall, stout stem. They add vertical interest to a garden and are often used to flank doorways or driveways. They, too, are the result of grafts. The rootstock is grown for around three years as a single stem, and all side shoots are removed. After the rootstock plant has reached the desired height, the scion is inserted below the bark of the rootstock stem.

- Any shoot that arises below the branches of a standard rose (such as from the main stem) is a sucker and should be removed.
- Standard roses are fragile and easily snap, so always stake them well using a small tree stake and ties.

ROSE GROWTH FORMS

Roses of different groups (see pp. 16–19) differ in their growth habits. Hybrid Tea and Floribunda roses of Group 1 usually have an open-centered bushy habit and quite stiff, upright-growing stems, while Group 1 Shrub roses tend to be larger-growing with a denser framework of thorny stems arising from the base of the plant and have a less formal appearance.

Group 2 roses often resemble more compact versions of Group 1 plants, with correspondingly smaller flowers, while roses in Group 3 are highly diverse in habit, ranging from the rather compact, rounded habit of Damask Portland roses to the more twiggy bushes of China roses and the rambling forms of Rubiginosas.

Group 4 roses all produce long shoots that need support: the growth of Ramblers tends to be more vigorous and pliable than that of Climbers, and with more stems arising from the base. Group 5 Ground Cover roses tend to be bushy, like low shrub roses, or have pliable rambler-like stems that root into the ground as they spread out.

The form of a rose helps determine if it will thrive when grown next to other plants in a mixed border.

Deadheading your roses regularly will encourage your plants to flower well through summer and into fall, providing superb season-long displays.

HOW TO GROW ROSES

Roses are glamorous plants that often take a starring role in the garden. Surprisingly, they will fare well for years, many with relatively little care. The key is to give them the best possible start—good site selection and planting are important (*see pp.26–33*)—and then provide regular seasonal attention, such as pruning and feeding. When things occasionally go wrong, problems are usually easily remedied because many roses are tough and forgiving.

SITE SELECTOR

Different species and cultivars of roses thrive in different situations, from full sun to part shade, from rich to poor soil, and so on. The key to success is choosing and planting a rose suited to the exact conditions at the site. If you don't have any open ground, don't worry: many roses will flourish for years in containers (see pp.42–43).

GRAVEL GARDEN

CONDITIONS Open, sunny sites with free draining, often poor soil, hot and dry in summer, and with little winter shelter.
WHAT TO LOOK FOR Tough, unfussy roses that form well-shaped, leafy shrubs.
ROSES TO TRY 'Ballerina', BONICA ('Meidomonac'), CENTRE STAGE ('Chewcreepy'), 'Flower Carpet Coral', *R. glauca*, *R. rugosa* 'Alba', *R. sericea*.

SUNNY BORDER NEXT TO A WALL OR FENCE

CONDITIONS South-facing sites in full sun, further heated in summer by reflections from a fence or wall and sheltered by the structure in winter.
WHAT TO LOOK FOR Shrub or climbing roses that enjoy heat, and that begin to flower before risk of frost has passed. Consider Noisette; Bourbon; Hybrid Musk; Tea and China roses; Modern Shrub roses, such as hybrids with *Rosa persica*; and some English roses.
ROSES TO TRY *R. banksiae* var. *banksiae* 'Lutea', 'Ballerina', *R. odorata* 'Bengal Crimson', 'Buff Beauty', 'Cornelia', 'Climbing Lady Hillingdon', 'Felicia', 'New Dawn', *R. odorata* 'Mutabilis', 'Perle d'Or', THE GENEROUS GARDENER ('Ausdrawn'), GERTRUDE JEKYLL ('Ausbord').

NORTH-FACING WALL OR FENCE

CONDITIONS Cool, part-shade, slow to warm in spring and out of summer heat; usually moist.
WHAT TO LOOK FOR Climbers that grow well with a few hours of sun per day. Avoid tender or early-flowering roses.
ROSES TO TRY 'Albertine', 'Félicité-Perpétue', 'Gardeners' Glory', 'Seagull', SUMMER WINE ('Korizont').

UNDER HIGH TREES

CONDITIONS Partially shaded (not deep shade), sheltered sites out of summer heat but with rooty soil that can be dry.
WHAT TO LOOK FOR Roses that thrive out of direct sun.
ROSES TO TRY 'Ballerina', BONICA ('Meidomonac'), 'Flower Carpet Coral', PARTRIDGE ('Korweirim'), *R. gallica* var. *officinalis, R. glauca, R. rugosa* 'Alba'.

ARCH OR ARBOR

CONDITIONS Variable, but with limited space to climb or ramble.
WHAT TO LOOK FOR Roses with scrambling stems that repeat flower to give a long season of interest; less vigorous Climbers and Hybrid Musk roses.
ROSES TO TRY 'Buff Beauty', 'Cornelia', DIZZY HEIGHTS ('Fryblissful'), 'Felicia' 'Gardeners' Glory', 'New Dawn'.

PERGOLA

CONDITIONS A range of aspects, often with multiple strong supports to climb.
WHAT TO LOOK FOR Climbers/ramblers with cascading growth, not too vigorous.
ROSES TO TRY 'Albertine', 'Alister Stella Gray', 'Céclie Brunner', 'Félicité-Perpétue', 'Gardeners' Glory', 'New Dawn', Open Arms ('Chewpixcel'), THE GENEROUS GARDENER ('Ausdrawn').

THROUGH A TREE

CONDITIONS Variable, but often shaded (at first), with poor root-filled soil. Plenty of room and strong support.
WHAT TO LOOK FOR Vigorous climbers and ramblers that need little care.
ROSES TO TRY 'Céclie Brunner', 'Félicité-Perpétue', 'Gardeners' Glory', 'Madame Alfred Carrière', 'Seagull,' SUMMER WINE ('Korizont').

FLOWERING HEDGE

CONDITIONS Variable, but often exposed, windy sites.
WHAT TO LOOK FOR Tough, bushy, dense roses that branch well or sucker freely, not fussy about pruning or deadheading.
ROSES TO TRY 'Charles de Mills', GOLDEN CELEBRATION ('Ausgold'), HOT CHOCOLATE ('Wekpaltlez'), *R. gallica* var. *officinalis, R. gallica* 'Versicolor', *R. rugosa* 'Alba'.

CUTTING GARDEN

CONDITIONS Sunny sites with little competition from other plants.
WHAT TO LOOK FOR Roses with shapely, well-presented, scented flowers that bloom profusely and display well.
ROSES TO TRY CHANDOS BEAUTY ('Harmisty'), CLARET ('Frykristal'), GERTRUDE JEKYLL ('Ausbord'), 'Just Joey', PURPLE TIGER ('Jacpurr').

Rose arches are a focal point in the summer garden. Choose cultivars that are vigorous enough to cover, but not overwhelm, their supports.

PLANTING PARTNERS

Roses are distinctive, long-flowering, and rewarding to grow, and many gardeners opt to showcase them in dedicated rose beds. However, many growers—especially those with restricted space—integrate roses with other plants. A wide range of roses can be grown in this way, underplanted with spring bulbs or alongside other shrubs with complementary foliage or coordinated flower colors.

When planting, think about the eventual height and floral density of the roses and the surrounding perennials.

PERENNIALS

Mixing roses with perennials is an effective planting strategy if your goal is to create a relaxed, flower-filled country- or cottage-style garden. Choose perennials that will not compete too intensely with the roses: these are typically plants with an airy, open habit, or those that bear slender spires of flowers. Classic choices include *Campanula persicifolia*, *Geranium sanguineum*, smaller *Nepeta*, *Alchemilla*, and asters. Also consider *Astrantia*, *Digitalis*, *Oenothera lindheimeri*, various *Salvia*, *Verbena bonariensis*, slender grasses such as *Stipa tenuissima* and some herbs. Be sure to allow sufficient space around each rose when planting. Consider planting roses as a group at the front or on a corner of the border, where the aspect is naturally more open and competition is reduced.

White roses here provide a calming backdrop, allowing the warm colors of the planting to shine.

SHRUBS

Most roses need plenty of light and space, so do not compete well against tall, vigorous shrubs. However, you can plant roses with small, dense shrubs that will stay within an allotted space: clipped evergreens such as *Buxus*, *Ilex crenata*, or *Santolina* work well. Also good are slender columns of Irish yew or fastigiate *Berberis*, such as *B. thunbergii* f. *atropurpurea* 'Helmond Pillar', that provide contrasting form. Lavender is often recommended as a partner, but be sure to trim it back well after flowering. Purple or gold-leaved *Cotinus* or *Sambucus* make effective backdrops, but allow enough growing space and prune them well every year.

Rose and lavender is a classic pairing, but be sure to allow sufficient space.

TOP TIP MAKE GROUP 3 OR GROUP 4 ROSES YOUR FIRST CHOICE FOR MIXED PLANTINGS—MANY ARE SOCIABLE AND EASY TO INTEGRATE WITH EXISTING SHRUBS.

CLIMBERS

Rambling and climbing roses can mix to great effect with other climbing plants to provide walls of flowers and foliage with long seasonal interest. Wall shrubs trained on to wires or trellis can act as living supports for climbing roses: try *Pyracantha*, *Ceanothus*, *Solanum crispum,* and *Abutilon*, all of which make excellent hosts.

Climbers with twining stems, leaves, and tendrils will scramble through a rose. *Clematis viticella* and *C. texensis* are ideal because they flower late and provide another hit of color amid fading roses. Also effective are *Jasminum officinale*, *Eccremocarpus scaber,* and species of *Lonicera*, *Passiflora*, and even *Wisteria* with vigorous rambling roses. Avoid *Clematis montana*, *Akebia,* and *Humulus*—they may swamp your roses.

Climbing roses are here paired beautifully with clematis.

Alliums have globe-shaped flower heads that work well with roses: they may also help to ward off aphids.

BULBOUS PLANTS

Bulbs have a life cycle perfectly suited for growing with roses. They bring ephemeral color in spring well before any roses come into leaf, and die back before roses peak, so do not compete for light and space. They are most useful for masking the bare lower stems of roses, particularly Group 1 roses. *Galanthus*, *Muscari*, *Crocus*, smaller daffodils and tulips, *Chionodoxa*, and *Scilla* are most suitable. If roses are not closely planted, try *Alliums* such as *hollandicum* 'Purple Sensation' or *christophii*, or even *Eremurus*, which has tall, slender spires that look great between shrub roses.

BUYING AND PLANTING ROSES

Roses are sold either as potted shrubs or as bare-root plants. Whichever you choose, good planting and aftercare are key to making sure that they establish well and fulfill their potential. Climbing and rambling roses need to be supported at planting time for them to grow successfully.

Bare-root plants are available in winter and early spring. Their roots should be carefully wrapped to prevent drying out.

FROM STORE TO SOIL

Roses growing in pots are available almost year-round, while dormant, leafless, bare-root roses are available only in winter and early spring. In general, there is more choice of cultivars among bare-root roses; they are easier to buy by mail order, and are often better value.

When choosing a potted rose, select a well-shaped, sturdy plant with leafy stems. Reject plants with signs of disease or pest damage. Bare-root plants should have healthy, well-wrapped roots and at least three cleanly cut stems of pencil thickness. Reject any with wrinkled bark or developed foliage. Potted roses can be planted at any time when the ground is not frozen, but bare-root roses should be planted only in winter to early spring. Before planting, soak the soil of the potted roses or stand bare-root plants in water for an hour.

YOU WILL NEED Spade • fork • cane • mycorrhizal fungi powder • mulch

1 Choose your site (see pp.26–27). If roses grew there previously, take steps to avoid replant disease (see p.46). Dig a hole about twice the width and depth of the pot or roots.
2 Add mycorrhizal inoculant powder (see p.46) to the hole following instructions on the package. This

promotes an association between the rose's roots and beneficial fungi.
3 Remove the pot (if there is one) and position the plant in the center of the hole. Lay a cane over the hole and use it to set the depth of

planting; the graft union (see p.22) should be 2 in (5 cm) below the final soil surface.
4 Backfill with soil then firm-in. Water well and mulch with manure or garden compost.

PLANTING CARE

If you are planting more than one rose bush, make sure to allow 3 ft (1 m) between plants as growing space. Keep the newly planted roses moist for the first year. Water roses planted from pots at least weekly. Bare-root roses must be watered every other day for the first month, then weekly thereafter. Don't apply any artificial fertilizers until the plants have produced their first flowers—you risk burning the new roots. Keep your roses clear of weeds and other vegetation so they can develop freely, and deal with any pests and disease promptly; severe attacks may indicate your plant is suffering stress.

New roses need generous watering; dry spring weather is becoming increasingly common, so be watchful for wilting leaves.

CLIMBING AND RAMBLING ROSES

Climbers and Ramblers are often trained along walls and fences or grown to disguise outbuildings. When planting these roses, make sure to position them beyond the rain shadow cast by the supporting structure. In practice, this means planting the rose at least 12–18 in (30–45 cm) away from the wall. If you plant within this limit, rainwater will not reach all of the roots, and footings of the wall or building may limit root growth.

Before planting, ensure that the supporting wires or trellis (see pp.40–41) are in place and sufficiently sturdy to support the rose when it reaches its full size and weight (dense flower heads can get very heavy). If training a Climber or Rambler through a tree, plant it under the tree canopy's outer edge, rather than next to the main trunk, and use canes to train shoots up to the branches.

Plant Climbers and Ramblers at a slight angle toward the support.

Firm in soil around the roots then tie the shoots to the support.

NEED TO KNOW
- The optimum time to plant roses is in early spring, when the risk of frost has passed, or in the fall, well before the first frosts, so the roots can establish before the plants become dormant over winter.
- Bare-root roses may arrive before you are ready to plant; store them temporarily by digging a shallow trench, covering the roots with soil, and firming in.
- Avoid buying cheap bare-root roses with wax-coated stems.

CARING FOR YOUR ROSES

Easy to please and generally undemanding to grow, roses repay good cultivation with impressive, long-lasting displays of flowers. The steps to success are simple: choose the right plant for the location (see *pp.32–33*); keep it well-fed and watered in times of drought; and observe good garden hygiene. If you stay on top of deadheading, you may be rewarded with repeated flushes of flowers for months.

In spring, add a mulch of well-rotted manure or garden compost around roses to feed them and to retain moisture.

TOOLS

Only a few general gardening tools are required, along with some basic materials, such as twine and wire to tie in Climbers, stakes to support taller plants, and labels to record the names of the roses you choose. Make sure to keep tools sharp and clean.

1 **PRUNERS** These are essential for deadheading and pruning. Bypass pruners are most versatile, while anvil pruners are better for removing dead wood.

2 **PRUNING SAW** These are occasionally needed when renovating older plants, particularly climbers with thick, woody stems.

3 **HAND FORK AND TROWEL** Use these to keep the soil around your roses weed- and debris-free, and to evenly spread out plant food and mulch.

4 **GLOVES** Hand protection is vital when tying-in Climbers and Ramblers, or removing old wood.

5 **HAND SPRAYER** This may be needed for the occasional application of fungicides and pesticides.

6 **WATERING CAN** This is the best and most sustainable way to water during dry spells. It is best to apply water directly at the roots.

SPRING FEED

Roses respond well to a spring feed. Spread a handful of granular plant food—one formulated specifically for roses—onto the soil just as the plant begins its spring growth. Work the food lightly into the soil surface with a hand fork and water it in if the ground is dry. Next, apply a 2-in (5-cm) mulch of rotted manure or garden compost

TOP TIP A HAND SPRAYER NEED NOT BE JUST FOR CHEMICALS: FILL IT WITH WATER AND SPRAY AT CLOSE RANGE TO DISLODGE APHID PESTS FROM ROSE BUDS.

over the soil, adjacent to the plant's stems. This will feed the rose and help lock in soil moisture. Feed any repeat-flowering roses again in early summer for best results.

Feed in spring with a handful of granular fertilizer.

REMOVING SUCKERS

Occasionally, grafted roses produce suckers—unbranched, vigorous shoots that arise below the soil from the rootstock, weakening top growth. Suckers appear quickly, and are usually obvious because their foliage differs in form, size, or color from that of your rose; if you are unsure, trace the sucker back to its point of origin. It is better to tear suckers off at the base by hand rather than cutting them back.

Use a hand trowel to excavate the soil to reveal the sucker's origin.

Tear off, rather than cut, the sucker: this will prevent its regrowth.

Individual faded flowers can be pinched off Hybrid Tea or Floribunda roses.

DEADHEADING

Removing dead or fading flowers from your rose is called deadheading. The technique promotes further flowering on roses that repeat bloom, keeps the plants looking tidy, and helps reduce disease. For roses that produce clusters of flowers, remove individual blooms as they fade, either by pinching them out or cutting them off with pruners. For solitary flowers (or if a whole head has faded) cut the flowering stem off above a leaf. Roses that flower only once a year do not need deadheading; unless they are unsightly, leave them to develop hips. For roses that repeat and have hips, retain a third of the faded flowers from the first flush, and do not deadhead the second.

When a full head of flowers has finished, cut it off just above a leaf node.

NEED TO KNOW

- Carry out a thorough spring clean before your roses come into leaf. Remove weeds and competing vegetation from around plants to reduce stress in summer.
- Regularly clear old fallen foliage from below and around roses. This debris may harbor diseases such as rust, blackspot, or mildew which can reinfect plants.
- Pick off any of last year's remaining rose leaves in early spring. In a mild winter, many may be retained and can carry rose diseases.

Deadheading will divert your rose's energy away from making hips, and toward producing more flowers. It also helps your garden look tidier.

PRUNING GROUP 1, 2, AND 3 ROSES

Most types of rose benefit from pruning. This selective cutting back of stems keeps plants healthy, stimulating new shoots and promoting better flowering. It prevents a build-up of old, diseased wood and improves air flow through plants, reducing disease problems. With most bush roses, the outcome of successful pruning is a more open-centred plant with well-spaced stems. Pruning is usually carried out in winter, or, for some types, such as a few Old Garden roses, after flowering in summer.

Pruning improves rose health. Cutting back hard will encourage the strongest growth.

MAKING CUTS

When pruning roses, always use clean, sharp secateurs to reduce the chances of spreading disease. Cuts stems above a healthy, outward-facing bud, ensuring that the cut slants away from the bud at an angle of 45 degrees. This helps shed rainwater from the cut surface, reducing the risk of rot setting in and killing the shoot. If no bud is visible where you want to cut the stems, go ahead anyway – the act of pruning will encourage shoots to form. Roses are tolerant, so don't be nervous of getting pruning wrong – your plant will soon recover.

GROUP 1: MODERN GARDEN BUSH ROSES

The aim of pruning Group 1 roses is to encourage flower-bearing side branches to develop from the main stems. Carry out the pruning in late winter. If you live in a cold, exposed area, an initial trim of 15–30cm (6–12in) in autumn can mitigate wind damage.

Start by cutting out dead, damaged, and diseased shoots at their base. Remove stems that rub against their neighbours. Next, cut stems as described below to an outward-facing bud (a bud that points away from the centre of the plant); this will reduce crowding of stems and result in an open-centred rose.

HYBRID TEA AND FLORIBUNDA ROSES

These roses tend to become leggy and leafless at the base, so it is best to avoid letting them grow too tall. Cut stems down to one third of their height, to an outward facing bud.

SHRUB ROSES (INCLUDING ENGLISH ROSES)

Cut the main stems to about one half of their length. The less you prune, the taller your plant will become. Then cut back side branches to 10cm (4in) from the main stem.

Hybrid Tea and Floribunda roses can be cut back quite hard, trimming to outward facing buds, as this recently planted example shows.

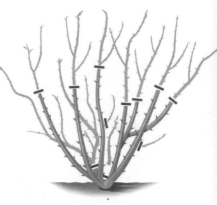

Cut stems by around half to one third and take out any dead or diseased growth at the base of the plant.

PRUNING STANDARDS

Standard roses need to be pruned quite hard in late winter (*pictured below*). The branches on top of the long stem should be kept short or the plant can become top-heavy.

- Aim for a rounded head; cut back branches by around two thirds to an outward-facing bud. Thin out older branches from the center to allow good air flow.
- For weeping standards, remove any upward-growing shoots as they arise.

Rosa QUEEN MOTHER ('Korquemu') flowers profusely with good pruning.

Rosa 'Ballerina' is one of the most popular and reliable of Group 2 roses.

GROUP 2: SMALL BUSH ROSES

These roses require only the lightest pruning, with the aim of promoting profuse summer flowering and maintaining plant vigor. Pruning should be carried out in late winter. Start by cutting out and removing dead, damaged, and diseased shoots at their base. Remove shoots that rub against their neighbors.

PATIO AND POLYANTHA ROSES These compact roses have bushy growth that often becomes twiggy and unproductive. Once plants are well established, gradually remove this twiggy material. Reduce leading shoots by one third back to a strong bud or side branch.

MINIATURE ROSES Pruning established plants encourages vigorous new shoots from the base. Reduce the weakest, oldest branches to a strong bud and cut out twiggy growth.

GROUP 3: OLD GARDEN ROSES

This large group includes diverse roses with different pruning regimes. As a general rule they should be pruned more lightly than Group 1 selections. The aim of pruning is to retain as much natural character as possible. When pruning an established rose, cut out and remove dead, damaged, and diseased shoots at their base. Remove shoots that rub against their neighbors.

ALBA, CENTIFOLIA, DAMASK, GALLICA, AND MOSS ROSES These roses flower just once a year and are best pruned after blooming ends in summer. This gives them maximum time to grow before flowering the following year. Remove weak growth and thin any crowded stems, then trim remaining shoots by one quarter.

BOURBON, HYBRID MUSK, AND HYBRID PERPETUAL ROSES These are repeat-flowering roses. They require light pruning in winter to prevent them from becoming too leggy. Remove the weakest oldest growth and reduce the longest shoots by around a third.

RUGOSA ROSES These repeat-flowering roses should be pruned in winter. Thin out the weakest growth and trim off any wayward stems.

CHINA AND TEA ROSES These repeat-flowering roses need a gentle touch. In winter, remove the oldest stem or two at the base to promote the formation of young shoots.

RUBIGINOSA, SPECIES, AND SPINOSISSIMA ROSES Roses in these groups flower just once a year. Prune them lightly in late winter, after the show of rose hips is over.

Group 3 roses seldom need hard pruning as they have a pleasing natural form.

Rosa rugosa benefits from a winter tidy to remove the weakest stems at ground level.

PRUNING GROUP 4 AND 5 ROSES

Free-spirited Ramblers usually flower just once a year and most require only minimal late-summer pruning. However, Climbers need more intensive pruning in winter, which is also the best time to train them to **their supports. Some Ground Cover roses grow rather like Ramblers with long, slender, flexible stems that need very little pruning other than to keep them within bounds.**

GROUP 4: CLIMBING ROSES AND RAMBLERS

The aim of pruning these roses is to encourage the production of more flowering stems and create a good branch structure. First, cut out dead, damaged, and diseased shoots, and those that rub together, at their bases.

CLIMBERS AND BOURSAULT AND NOISETTE ROSES

These roses flower on side branches—ones that arise from main stems—produced in the current year. Main stems trained close to the horizontal will provide numerous side branches. In winter, prune side branches to around 4–6 in (10–15 cm) and tie in any new shoots. Retain no more than six main stems, removing the oldest first. If there is just one, reduce it by around half; it may not re-shoot if cut back hard.

RAMBLERS Most of these roses flower just once a year, on growth made in that year. Prune in late summer after flowers and hips have faded. Keep plants in bounds by cutting out one third of the oldest stems at the base; retain no more than six. Shorten side shoots to 6 in (15 cm) and tie in young new shoots. Leave repeat-flowering selections or ramblers in trees unpruned.

Horizontal wires are the best way to support wall-trained roses.

SUPPORTING CLIMBERS AND RAMBLERS

Many climbing plants cling to walls and fences using tendrils, twining stems, or clinging roots. Roses instead rely on their thorns to hold their branches in place.

Providing a solid framework to support your Climbers and Ramblers will help them thrive and make them more manageable. The least obtrusive option is a set of parallel horizontal wires affixed to a wall by vine eyes. The alternative is a wooden trellis, obelisk, or tripod. Tie the stems to the supports with green garden twine (not wire, which will cut into living tissue). Tie twine neatly—birds will pick at any loose ends. If using trellis, do not weave stems through the structure as they may destroy it as they grow; simply tie the stems to one face of the trellis.

Move outer stems as close to horizontal as possible, tying them in firmly to wires.

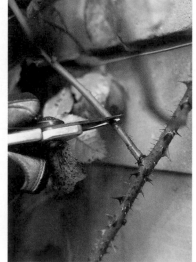

Prune side branches to an outward bud 4–6 in (10–15 cm) from the main branch.

Arch outer branches close to the horizontal and fan out and tie in the more upright inner branches to fill the space.

Ramblers can be carefree but still need attaching to supporting trees.

TRAINING

When buying a Climber or Rambler at a nursery or garden center, choose one with three or four main stems. The two outer stems will be arched over and trained horizontally, while the inner stem(s) will initially be grown vertically or diagonally, and later fanned out to cover available space. Training stems to the horizontal encourages the production of side branches, and it is these that bear the flowers.

As your rose grows, bend the stems down and tie them in tightly to wires or trellis to prevent them springing back. This will initiate more side shoots. Repeat the process until horizontal stems occupy all the available wall space. If you are growing a climber on an obelisk, tripod, or pillar, train the stems carefully around the support in a spiral pattern to promote better flowering all over the structure.

If growing a Rambler or Climber through a tree, plant it under the tree canopy's outer edge and use canes to train shoots up to the branches. Then loosely tie the young stems to tree branches once they reach the canopy.

GROUP 5: GROUND COVER ROSES

These low-growing roses need only light pruning to keep them within bounds. This promotes good flowering and the vigorous growth that provides dense cover. In late winter, cut out dead, damaged, diseased, and rubbing shoots.

Rosa SUFFOLK (**'Kormixal'**) provides good ground cover but needs little pruning.

For shrubby selections with low but upright growth, reduce the strong leading shoots by one third and side shoots to two or three buds. To rejuvenate overgrown plants, simply prune them back to 4 in (10 cm) from the ground.

For ground-hugging selections with prostrate stems (which root-in as they spread), trim shoots in summer after flowering if they get too long. To rejuvenate plants, prune back to 4 in (10 cm) from the original base in late winter.

TOP TIP RATHER THAN USING A LADDER TO PRUNE OUT-OF-REACH STEMS, TRY A LONG-HANDLED TREE PRUNER. BE AWARE THAT CLIMBERS AND RAMBLERS CAN BE PARTICULARLY THORNY, SO MAKE SURE YOU WEAR STURDY GLOVES WHEN HANDLING THEIR STEMS.

ROSES IN CONTAINERS

You can enjoy a dazzling display of roses whatever the size of your outdoor space by growing plants in containers. Even if you have a big garden, growing roses in pots is worthwhile because you can move fragrant cultivars close to doors and windows in the summer to make the most of their scent.

Some compact and spreading varieties have been specially bred for use in pots, while others—even certain Climbers and Shrub roses—will also perform well for years in containers, as long as suitable pots are used and plant care is consistent throughout the summer.

GETTING STARTED

Roses are thirsty, hungry plants that send out long, spreading roots to harvest moisture and nutrients from the soil. If you wish to grow roses in pots, choosing a container of sufficient width and depth is vital. Compact patio roses will need pots at least 12 in (30 cm) deep and across, but vigorous types, such as shrub roses and English roses (many of which can grow very successfully in pots), need larger containers at least 18 in (45 cm)

deep. Small climbing roses will require bigger pots still in order to remain viable for a number of years— 24 x 24 in (60 x 60 cm) at a minimum.

Roses prefer their roots to be cool, so avoid plastic pots that provide little insulation and allow the soil to warm up excessively in direct sunlight. Terra-cotta or concrete pots have better thermal properties and are also more stable in windy conditions.

Figure out where you are going to place your potted roses. They will

flower best in full sun, although some will tolerate a little shade for part of the day. The ideal location is one where the top growth is in the sun, and the pot is at least partly in shade to keep the roots cool. Position the container before you plant your rose because the filled pot will be heavy and hard to move. Do not let the soil in the container dry out or become waterlogged (*see right*).

The dimensions of a pot must be large enough to allow for years of growth.

POTTING UP YOUR ROSE

Roses need a potting mix that can supply nutrients and moisture through summer. Multipurpose mixes become exhausted after around six weeks; a better choice for long-term container use is a potting mix containing some garden soil. Add some well-rotted manure to boost water-holding potential and nutrient content. Bare-root roses should be planted in winter (see pp.22–23), but container-grown roses can be planted out at almost any time—just avoid hot or frosty days. Make sure to use a pot that has drainage holes, and add a 2–4 in (5–10 cm) layer of broken crocks or shingle at the bottom to aid drainage. Pay attention to planting depth: the union between rootstock and top growth should be just below the soil surface. Firm the potting mix in carefully around the roots, but take care not to overfill; the surface should be about 2 in (5 cm) below the rim of the pot, so you can easily give the plant a thorough soaking.

Add a layer of broken crocks or shingle before filling the pot with potting mix.

Allow some space in the pot above the potting mix for watering.

WATERING AND FEEDING

Potted roses will soon let you know if they are not happy. Water-stressed plants will wilt visibly and develop diseases such as mildew and blackspot (see pp.44–45). To keep your roses healthy, ensure that the soil is always moist, but not waterlogged; regularly check the water content of the potting mix by pushing your fingertip ½ in (1 cm) below the surface and water if it feels dry. You will need to water daily in the summer, more in very hot weather.

In spring, sprinkle granular rose fertilizer on the potting mix surface; thereafter, feed the plants every other week throughout the summer with a balanced liquid feed. Every subsequent spring, replace the top 2–4 in (5–10 cm) of old potting mix with fresh material, adding granular feed and topping with a manure mulch. Prune potted roses in the same way as those in the ground (see pp.38–41).

Raise potted roses on pot stands in winter to maintain good drainage.

PERFECT ROSES FOR POTS

Many roses will grow in containers, but it is best to avoid large, vigorous types, such as Ramblers and strong-growing Climbers; larger Bush roses may also struggle when their roots are confined. The safest choices are Group 1 roses, especially Patio and Polyantha types. Less vigorous roses in Groups 1 and 3 also tend to fare well in pots, as do many English roses. Some Group 4 roses can do well, and Group 5 plants need a large pot but can be spectacular, spilling from an urn or planter. When starting out, try one of these container favorites:

Rosa 'Ballerina' • 'Perle d'Or' • 'Flower Carpet Coral' • HAPPY DAYS ('Harquad') • LADY OF SHALLOT ('Ausnyson') • THE GENEROUS GARDENER ('Ausdrawn') • Surrey ('Korlanum')

The dense spreading habit of the Polyantha *Rosa* 'Ballerina' makes it ideal for containers.

PESTS AND DISEASES

Most modern roses remain free of pests and diseases when grown well in good conditions. However, problems can occur, especially in periods of extreme weather. Keep an eye on your plants so you can spot problems early; most can then be dealt with by changing their growing conditions, but other measures are available if the situation worsens.

BLACKSPOT

SYMPTOMS Rounded black patches on foliage, connecting in severe cases. Leaves yellow before dropping off early.
CAUSE A fungal disease that spreads when foliage is wet.
REMEDY Choose resistant cultivars and feed them in summer. Water during the day, not evening; remove worst-affected leaves. Fungicides are a last resort.

ROSE DOWNY MILDEW

SYMPTOMS Purple patches on stems and upper surfaces of leaves, often causing foliage to yellow and then fall.
CAUSE A fungus-like organism that is most common during spells of wet weather, so worst in spring and fall.
REMEDY Remove infected material and try to improve air circulation. Avoid wetting leaves when watering.

ROSE POWDERY MILDEW

SYMPTOMS White powdery mold on foliage, buds, and stems that causes distorted growth and flowering.
CAUSE A fungus that spreads in humid conditions, and on plants that are too dry. Worst in wet springs and dry summers.
REMEDY Cut out affected shoots and improve air circulation. Plant resistant roses. Fungicides are a last resort.

RUST

SYMPTOMS Orange or black spots on foliage, orange spots on stems. Leaves likely to drop early.
CAUSE A fungal disease to which many modern roses are more or less immune.
REMEDY Cut out any affected growth in spring, then clear infected material in the fall. Choose resistant roses.

RED SPIDER MITE

SYMPTOMS Leaves yellow-mottled with fine webbing on shoots, especially in hot, dry weather. Foliage may fall early.
CAUSE Tiny sap-sucking mites found on the undersides of leaves; this greenhouse pest is found outside in hot summers.
REMEDY Wetting foliage can reduce the problem. Try biological control, or as a last resort, pesticides.

APHIDS

SYMPTOMS New shoots and buds are covered in small green or reddish bugs, distorting growth and causing black mold.
CAUSE Sap-sucking bugs damage plant growth and produce honeydew, which promotes the growth of black mold.
REMEDY Mild infestations can be ignored and left to natural predation. Otherwise, squash or dislodge with a hand sprayer.

LEAF-ROLLING SAWFLY

SYMPTOMS In spring or early summer, leaves roll into tubes, usually sheltering a green caterpillar within.
CAUSE The foliage curls when a female sawfly secretes chemicals into a leaf before laying her eggs.
REMEDY If infestation is light, pick off leaves or squash tubes to kill larvae; do not remove too many leaves.

ROSE SAWFLY

SYMPTOMS Leaves are devoured in summer to their main veins by conspicuously spotted caterpillars.
CAUSE Rose sawfly females lay eggs on rose stems; the eggs hatch and larvae begin to feed on the leaves.
REMEDY Remove all visible larvae. Use a contact insecticide only if the infestation is persistent.

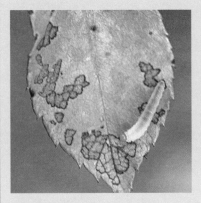

ROSE SLUG SAWFLY

SYMPTOMS Leaves develop irregular brown patches; their lower surfaces (usually) are consumed by a greenish, translucent, slug-like caterpillar.
CAUSE Larvae of the rose slug sawfly feast on foliage in summer.
REMEDY Check roses regularly and pick off visible larvae. Use a contact insecticide only in extreme cases.

LEAFHOPPERS

SYMPTOMS Leaves become speckled above, especially in hot weather; some leaves may turn brown and fall in severe cases.
CAUSE Tiny white insects suck the sap from plant tissue; they can be seen jumping off when disturbed.
REMEDY Damage is generally light and can be tolerated.

PROBLEM SOLVING

While most pests and diseases are relatively easy to detect (*see p.44–45*), the causes of some problems are less obvious. Plants may underperform due to poor or changed growing conditions—for example, a site that was once ideal may become shaded or overgrown. Problems below the soil, such as poor nutrition or rose replant disease, are even harder to spot, but once identified can be remedied.

Fast, healthy growth and development lets roses outpace any damage caused by pests and diseases.

Replant disease makes new plantings struggle and eventually die.

ROSE REPLANT DISEASE

This problem affects roses and others in the rose family, including fruit trees. Roses planted in ground where others previously grew will often fail to thrive, putting on weak growth, both above and below the soil. This effect can last for up to ten years at a site, making it a serious problem if you have dedicated rose beds because it makes it hard to replace occasional failed plants.

The causes of replant disease are not fully understood but are thought to be linked to the buildup of pathogens, notably nematodes (tiny wormlike creatures), and fungi in the soil. Horticulturalists have proposed that newly planted roses, which have small and fragile root systems, may be unable to cope with the existing high pathogen load. To avoid rose replant disease, the existing planting soil must be swapped for fresh (*see box, right*).

SOIL SWAP

To avoid replant disease, dig out and remove the soil that surrounded the root system of the old rose; a volume 32 in (80 cm) across and 16 in (40 cm) deep is usually enough. Fill the hole with fresh topsoil and add some well-rotted manure when planting the new rose. Add mycorrhizal inoculant to the soil according to instructions on the package; this contains fungi that establish a symbiotic relationship with the rose roots. This partnership helps roots take up water and nutrients and protects against pathogens left behind in the soil.

Threadlike mycorrhizal fungi are beneficial to roses.

IS THE SITE THE PROBLEM?

Unfavorable environmental conditions will cause your roses to grow weakly, produce few small flowers, or become susceptible to pests and diseases. The most common issues are:

TOO MUCH COMPETITION Adjacent plants can compete with roses for space, light, and nutrients. Cut back branches impinging on the rose and cut through any invading roots with a spade.

TOO WET Roses do not tolerate waterlogged soils. If the site is regularly saturated, lift and replant the roses. In wet gardens, grow roses in a raised bed or container.

TOO SHADED Roses need plenty of light; plant them in a spot that receives several hours of sunlight per day.

Some roses will integrate well into mixed borders but others need a bit of space around them to thrive.

Use a soil test kit to check pH: roses are easy-going but extreme conditions can cause issues.

YELLOWING FOLIAGE

If your roses develop pale yellow leaves and there are no signs of pests or diseases, the cause may be chlorosis, which is often the result of low nutrient levels. Roses in containers are most susceptible because they quickly exhaust their potting mix; repotting and regular feeding will solve their problem.

Roses usually thrive in acid or alkaline soils, but ground with extreme pH values can cause chlorosis, so it may be worth buying a soil test kit. Strongly acidic soils can have their pH raised by applying lime. If you have very chalky soil, grow your roses in raised beds.

Other nutrient deficiencies can also result in chlorosis, but go easy if applying fertilizer—too much may result in similar symptoms.

ROSE BALLING

Rose blooms may fail to open after flower buds are exposed to heavy rain. The outer petals rot and meld together, preventing opening; if sunshine follows rain, these petals dry, forming a brown ball. Sometimes it is possible to tease open the flowers by peeling away outer petals. Roses with tight double blooms are particularly prone; the pale pink Bourbon rose 'Souvenir de Malmaison' is a regular victim, seeming to flower just as the heavens open.

Rose balling occurs after a period of wet weather.

MAKING MORE ROSES

A cost-effective way to fill your garden with roses is to propagate rather than buy plants. There are a number of propagation methods, of which the simplest and most suitable for home gardeners is to take hardwood cuttings. These may succeed with little effort or care outside, without needing a greenhouse or even a windowsill. Other techniques may be more suitable for certain types of rose, for example, Climbers and Ramblers respond well to layering and roses that naturally form suckers can be divided.

Take hardwood cuttings from stems that are firm and woody.

PROPAGATING FROM HARDWOOD CUTTINGS

Most roses sold by nurseries and garden centers are products of bud grafting (see p.22); few are grown on their own roots. When you take a hardwood cutting from grafted rose, you are propagating only the above-ground portion (the original scion) and encouraging it to form its own roots. The resulting plants are often slower growing than grafted ones, but have the slight advantage of not producing suckers. Cuttings are initially quite delicate, so take plenty to give yourself the best chance of success. Some roses, such as Ramblers, can be propagated easily by this method; others, such as Hybrid Teas, may prove trickier.

TAKING CUTTINGS

Take cuttings in the fall, just after leaf fall, when new growth has become firm and woody (rather than soft and pale green). Look for healthy stems that are around the thickness of a pencil; they should be at least 12 in (30 cm) long.

You can break off any thorns to make handling easier. Use a clean, sharp knife or pruners to remove the tip of the stem and any old flower heads and leaves. Cut the stem into lengths of at least 6 in (15 cm). The cut at the base of each length must be straight and made just below a bud; the cut at the top of the section should be just above the uppermost bud, and made so that it slants away from the bud.

Prepare an area outdoors to receive the cuttings. Dig over a small bed in a warm, sheltered part of the garden, and improve the soil by adding garden compost. Lightly firm the soil and then dig a narrow trench. Pour a layer of sand into the base of the trench. Apply hormone rooting powder or gel to the bases of your cuttings, following instructions on the product. Insert the cuttings upright into the trench about 6 in (15 cm) apart, leaving about two-thirds of their length above ground. Firm the soil around them and water in.

Insert the prepared cuttings into a sand-filled trench in a dedicated bed outdoors.

Cut the top of the stem just above a viable bud.

The cuttings will start to grow new shoots from buds in spring.

Leave the cuttings to grow and develop healthy roots for one year.

Lift the cuttings and move them to their final positions, watering in well.

AFTERCARE

Once cuttings are in the soil, a callus (mass of soft tissue) will form over the cut end that is below ground. Roots will develop from the callus, and the cuttings will sprout, producing leaves in spring. Pinch off any flower buds that may develop (producing blooms wastes the plant's energies). Leave the cuttings in place for a full year—do not be tempted to move them earlier because it takes time for their roots to develop. Lift the cuttings that have developed well in the fall and plant them in improved soil in their intended positions (see p.32). Don't expect all your cuttings to strike; some are sure to fail.

Tall-growing roses, Climbers, and Ramblers can be propagated by layering.

Rosa gallica and others that form suckering thickets can be propagated by division.

Seeds from the hips of Species roses can be used for propagation.

OTHER TECHNIQUES

SEMI-RIPE CUTTINGS This method is similar to taking hardwood cuttings, but cuttings are taken in late summer from green side shoots that are just becoming woody. Insert 4in (10cm) lengths of stem into pots of growing mix. Put these pots into a propagator to maintain humidity, and place in a greenhouse or on a sunny windowsill. Cuttings should be ready for planting out in spring.

LAYERING This works for roses with long, flexible stems—Climbers, Ramblers, and tall Group 3 roses. In late summer, bend a stem to the soil that you have improved with compost. Remove a few leaves, cover the stem with soil, and peg it down with a metal hoop. Once well rooted, detach from the parent plant. Some Ground Cover roses do this naturally.

DIVISION This is useful for roses already growing on their own roots and which sucker naturally, such as *Rosa rugosa* and *R. gallica* cultivars. Detach rooted suckers in winter and plant in prepared soil.

SEED Only rose species can be grown from seed. The seeds should be chilled in a fridge for several weeks to break their dormancy before they are planted. They may then take a year to germinate. Do not bother to sow seed of hybrid roses; the resulting plants will be highly varied and inferior to their parents.

Rosa **HOT CHOCOLATE ('Wekpaltlez')** is a superbly colored Floribunda rose. It bears heads of highly scented flowers through summer and fall.

GROUP 1: MODERN GARDEN BUSH ROSES

This varied collection of roses includes some of the most up-to-date cultivars, as well as many of the best-known garden roses of all. Most members of the group will repeat flower, providing blooms, and often wonderful perfume, all season. In this group you will find plants for dedicated rose gardens, for mixing in borders with other shrubs and perennials, and roses for cutting and bringing indoors. Some also grow well in pots.

ABSOLUTELY FABULOUS

This free-flowering rose has been popular since its launch, winning awards for its generous displays of double blooms. Its flowers soften in color as they age, resulting in multihued clusters of gold, butter-yellow, and eventually pale primrose. Easy to grow, it has a long season, lasting through summer and fall and is a great choice for a rose garden or a mixed border.

CULTIVAR NAME 'Wekvossutono'
ROSE TYPE Group 1, Floribunda
FLOWERING Repeats in summer and fall
FLOWER SIZE 3¼–4 in (8–10 cm) across, held in clusters
FLOWER SCENT Strong, sweet, clove perfume
VIGOR Strong
DISEASE RESISTANCE Excellent
HARDINESS Around −4°F (−20°C)

Plant this vigorous rose for sweet scent and generous flowers.

FEATURES

This American-bred rose was awarded Rose of the Year in 2010 by the British Association of Rose Breeders, and has proved to be a great garden favorite; it is easy to grow and tolerant of hot, dry summers.

The double flowers never stop coming; they appear in large, showy clusters from early summer until fall and are strongly clove-scented. Individually, blooms are rounded and variable in both size and color—they open golden-yellow, then fade gradually to soft primrose, often resulting in multihued clusters. The plant is compact, reaching 3 ft (1 m) in height, with glossy green foliage that remains unblemished thanks to good disease resistance. It can bear attractive orange hips at the end of the season.

GARDEN USES

Absolutely Fabulous is an easygoing rose, tolerant of a range of sites, as long as they are well drained. Its shrubby, compact, rounded habit makes it ideal for a rose garden, but it will thrive in mixed borders if competition from its neighbors is kept under control. Full sun suits it best but it also performs well in part-shade as long as it gets some sun during the day. It is a contender for containers and has a place in the cutting garden because the blooms last well in water. It also makes a good standard rose.

CARE AND MAINTENANCE

Vigorous and sturdy, this Floribunda rose is straightforward to keep and tolerant of poorer soils. A good dose of granular plant food in spring along with a mulch of well-rotted manure should keep it in healthy growth through the year. During summer, once flowering has started, keep deadheading regularly to promote the development of more flowers. Pick up and remove any fallen petals to reduce disease risk. Watch out for aphids on new growth and rub them off as they appear. Prune in winter as for all Group 1 roses (see p.38).

ALSO TRY

If you are looking for other yellow Floribunda roses, try the following:
- **R. 'Chinatown'** is a tall-growing rose with huge, showy blooms that are often tinged pink at their edges. The flowers are sweetly scented.
- **R. Golden Wedding ('Arokris')** (pictured below) has rich yellow flowers all summer; these contrast perfectly with the dark foliage.

AMBER QUEEN

A fine Floribunda rose producing large, scented, double blooms in a glowing apricot-orange color, this cultivar has a low, compact habit and lush foliage to add to its appeal. Factor-in a reliable habit of repeat flowering into fall and dependable disease resistance, and it is easy to see why many growers regard this rose as a winner, especially where space is limited.

CULTIVAR NAME 'Harroony'
ROSE TYPE Group 1, Floribunda
FLOWERING Repeats in summer and fall
FLOWER SIZE 4–4¾ in (10–12 cm) across, held in clusters
FLOWER SCENT Spiced fragrance
VIGOR Average
DISEASE RESISTANCE Good
HARDINESS Around −4°F (−20°C)

FEATURES

This Floribunda rose has remained popular since its introduction by British breeder Harkness Roses in 1984. It is a compact, bushy plant that can reach a height of around 32 in (80 cm). Its foliage is lush: the large leaves are flushed red when young, becoming dark green when mature, while the stems are armed with red thorns. AMBER QUEEN's blooms are held in clusters of up to seven flowers. They are well perfumed and visually appealing: individual petals are elegantly cup-shaped and slightly ruffled. They take on a glowing apricot-orange color as they open, fading slightly to yellow as they age. This rose repeats well through summer and has good disease resistance, seldom troubled by problems when growing well.

GARDEN USES

AMBER QUEEN is a compact rose, ideal for the front of borders or narrow beds beside a path, but take care to plant it away from overhanging or competing plants. Low-growing perennials, such as *Geranium sanguineum* and *Alchemilla mollis,* make good neighbors. It could even be used as a hedging rose, forming a low, thorny boundary. The clusters of shapely flowers last well in water and are freely and quickly produced after cutting, making this rose a sound choice for a cutting border. Its compact habit also means that it should adapt well to growing in a container.

CARE AND MAINTENANCE

This rose prefers a sheltered position on a humus-rich, well-drained soil. Give it a good start in spring by applying granular rose fertilizer and mulching with well-rotted manure. This will keep it growing strongly and flowering well through the season. Once flowering has started, deadhead regularly: new flowers will soon appear. You can cut out individual blooms from the clusters to keep displays looking fresh and well-balanced. Keep an eye out for signs of blackspot (see *p.44*), especially during hot, dry periods and remove affected leaves; rub off any aphids that appear (see *p.44*). Prune AMBER QUEEN in winter as for all Group 1 roses (see *p.38*).

AMBER QUEEN's compact size makes it perfect for the front of a border.

BLUE FOR YOU

If you enjoy flowers with unusual colors, this distinctive cultivar is one to consider. With masses of sweetly scented white-eyed flowers that fade gradually from purple to blue-mauve, it is an excellent disease-resistant, modern, Floribunda rose. Its display lasts well through summer and into fall, and suits rose borders, mixed plantings, and large containers.

CULTIVAR NAME 'Pejamblu'
ROSE TYPE Group 1, Floribunda
FLOWERING Repeats in summer and fall
FLOWER SIZE 2¼–2¾ in (6–7 cm) across, held in clusters
FLOWER SCENT Sweet violet-like fragrance
VIGOR Average
DISEASE RESISTANCE Good
HARDINESS −4°F (−20°C)

FEATURES

True blue roses do not occur in nature, but the efforts of horticulturalists have produced a number of bluish-hued flowers. BLUE FOR YOU was raised by breeder Peter James and introduced in 2007. Its double- or semi-double flowers are dark purple when they emerge from pointed buds; they become more cupped with age while turning blue-mauve. The blooms have near-white hearts, decorated with a central boss of golden stamens, and are held in large showy clusters. Flowers repeat reliably through the summer and have a sweet perfume. Orange hips may develop in the fall if the last flush of flowers is not deadheaded.

GARDEN USES

BLUE FOR YOU grows as a rounded bush to a height of around 3 ft (1 m) but also makes a good standard. It is impressively long-flowering and sufficiently vigorous to be teamed with other plants in color-themed combinations—it looks great in a silvery-blue mixed border of *Nepeta* (catmint), *Salvia yangii* (Russian sage), and *Caryopteris*. This rose is also happy in a large container or in a dedicated rose border or island bed.

CARE AND MAINTENANCE

With few thorns, this rose is easy to handle and generally trouble-free. Feed well in spring by applying a handful of granular fertilizer and add manure or garden compost. Allow adequate space around each rose in mixed plantings. Aphids can be a problem if present in large numbers (see p.45) and should be removed by hand if possible. Prune as other Group 1 roses (see pp.38).

Abundant semi-double blooms in a soft lilac pink give this rose great appeal.

ALSO TRY

Try these Floribunda roses for alternative takes on bluish color:
- *Rosa* LILAC WINE ('Dicmulti') is a vigorous, well-scented Floribunda rose with rosette-shaped blooms opening blue-lilac and fading to pink.
- *R.* EYES FOR YOU ('Pejbigeye') is from the same breeding as BLUE FOR YOU. It has scented semi-double lilac-blue flowers, in this case with darker centers to each.
- *R.* LAVENDER ICE ('Tan04249') (pictured above) bears clusters of large, rosette-formed, lightly scented flowers of antique pinkish lavender above dark foliage.

CHANDOS BEAUTY

This outstanding **Hybrid Tea** rose is one of the best introductions of its kind in recent years. An asset to any garden, it flowers strongly through summer and fall and its large, double blooms of delicate, creamy apricot-pink produce a sensational fruity scent. It is robust and easy to please, with upright, disease-resistant growth, and is well suited to cutting.

CULTIVAR NAME 'Harmisty'
ROSE TYPE Group 1, Hybrid Tea
FLOWERING Repeats in summer and fall
FLOWER SIZE 4–4¾ in (10–12 cm) across, held singly
FLOWER SCENT Exceptionally fragrant
VIGOR Strong
DISEASE RESISTANCE Good
HARDINESS Around −4°F (−20°C)

FEATURES

Introduced in 2005 by Harkness Roses, this Hybrid Tea rose is justly popular. The flowers are large and beautifully formed with a high-centered, spiral structure. They are warm yet delicate in color—soft apricot pink, with an arresting golden glow that is set off by the plant's glossy dark green foliage. The plant is relatively tall, reaching around 4 ft (1.2 m), and so offers up its flowers at the perfect height to appreciate their fruity scent. It is repeat flowering, so the show continues all summer and into the fall.

GARDEN USES

Robust and vigorous, CHANDOS BEAUTY delivers in a range of garden settings. It likes a sunny site but will grow well in east- or west-facing borders. You can plant it in a rose garden, but it also succeeds with other garden plants in mixed borders, so long as it has adequate space around it. Its height means that it mixes well with a range of other species: try it alongside silver-leaved perennials or white flowers, where its subtle but glowing blooms inject warmth into a pale color scheme. Alternatively, plant it behind a row of lavender to create an intensely perfumed border. Another suitable place for this rose is the cutting garden—the flowers are so spectacular that it is worth growing several plants to fill vases indoors.

This elegant rose is ideal in borders or grown for cutting.

CARE AND MAINTENANCE

CHANDOS BEAUTY is easy to grow and, given good growing conditions, will repay you with a succession of flowers all summer. Its robust constitution also means that as long as its basic needs are met, it should not suffer from disease. Treat it as you would any other rose: apply granular plant food in spring, and mulch with well-rotted manure; then feed with a rose fertilizer throughout the growing season. Keep deadheading your plant through summer and flowers will continue into the fall. Make sure the rose never gets too crowded within mixed plantings. Prune in winter as for all Group 1 roses (see p.38).

CLARET

This cultivar bears large, shapely, dark crimson, semi-double flowers that mark it out as a winner both in the garden and as a cut flower. The delicately scented, velvety blooms open from near-black buds and gradually lighten with age; they will repeat all summer long if the plant is deadheaded regularly. Claret is fairly trouble-free and able to thrive in most soil types.

CULTIVAR NAME 'Frykristal'
ROSE TYPE Group 1, Hybrid Tea
FLOWERING Repeats through summer
FLOWER SIZE 4¾in (12 cm) or more across, held singly
FLOWER SCENT Light fruity perfume
VIGOR Average
DISEASE RESISTANCE Good
HARDINESS Around −4°F (−20°C)

Lush, velvety flowers sit atop sturdy stems with prominent thorns.

FEATURES

Bred by Gareth Fryer and launched in 2005, this dramatic cultivar is one to consider if you are looking for a classic red rose. Petals of the darkest red emerge from large pointed buds. As the flowers open, their elegant form emerges—high centered with a perfect swirl of velvety petals. The dark red hue lightens as the semi-double flowers develop and become more cup shaped. The blooms have a fruity perfume and are held on stout stems that reach a height of around 32 in (80 cm). The foliage is glossy and mid-green in hue. Prompt deadheading results in repeat flushes through summer. Rough spells of weather seem not to trouble the flowers.

GARDEN USES

The bushes of this rose are more upright than spreading, making it easy to accommodate in most gardens. Give it a sunny place in a rose border or try pairing it with small spring bulbs or low-growing perennials, such as smaller geraniums, violas, or alpine phlox, but avoid too much competition directly around or above the rose. If you have an area set aside for growing cut flowers, this rose is certainly one to consider for its dramatic indoor appeal.

CARE AND MAINTENANCE

CLARET is an easy rose to keep. Remember to give it a good dressing of rose fertilizer in spring, and then mulch with well-rotted manure.

Regular deadheading is key to ensuring repeated flushes of flowers through the summer. Always remove dead and diseased growth and cut back as for other Group 1 roses when pruning in winter; this rose gets few disease problems, but watch for

ALSO TRY

Other red Hybrid Tea roses that bring drama to a garden include:
- *Rosa* CARRIS ('Harmanna') (pictured above) has large, richly scented blooms.
- *R.* 'Mister Lincoln' is a vigorous, tall rose with strongly scented, velvety-red blooms.
- *R.* THINKING OF YOU ('Frydandy') has crimson flowers with a good scent. It is a tidy, compact plant.

white deposits on flowers and shoots in summer, which may signal powdery mildew (see p.44). Deal with aphids as you spot them (see p.45). Prune as for all Group 1 roses (see p.38).

EASY GOING

This plant is a great choice if you are new to growing roses. Tough and reliable, it adds floral impact to rose gardens and borders and is highly resistant to disease, especially blackspot. Once established, it provides years of color: its clusters of large, ruffled, apricot-orange, double flowers are produced in flushes throughout summer, held above healthy, glossy green foliage.

CULTIVAR NAME 'Harflow'
ROSE TYPE Group 1, Floribunda
FLOWERING Produces flushes through summer
FLOWER SIZE 4–4¾ in (10–12 cm) across, held in clusters
FLOWER SCENT Light sweet perfume
VIGOR Strong
DISEASE RESISTANCE Excellent
HARDINESS −4°F (−20°C)

FEATURES

Easy Going was introduced in 1998 by Harkness Roses after it had been found growing as a sport on another rose. It soon gained a reputation for being among the easiest and most reliable of Floribunda roses, with excellent resistance to blackspot and other diseases and a good repeat-flowering habit. The blooms are warm in hue—golden-apricot aging to soft orange—with a mild, pleasant fragrance. They open in small clusters from shapely buds. The flowers are initially high-centered but become more open and ruffled in appearance as they age. The foliage is remarkably glossy and healthy-looking, while the plant itself is quite densely branched, with an upright form that reaches a height of around 36 in (90 cm).

GARDEN USES

Easy Going prefers a sunny, open situation, but will tolerate some shade for part of the day. It does well in most soils as long as they are well drained. With its notable disease resistance it is a good choice for planting in groups in rose borders, but it also excels in combination with other plants. Spring bulbs such as *Muscari*, *Chionodoxa,* and *Scilla* will carpet the ground before roses come into growth, while lower-growing *Geranium*, *Alchemilla,* and *Nepeta* complement the rose without reducing performance.

CARE AND MAINTENANCE

As its name suggests, this rose is easygoing, with no special care needs. Remain vigilant though, especially in exceptionally hot, dry or cool, wet years, when plants will naturally be under more stress. Prune in winter as for all Group 1 roses (see p.38).

Lush amber-gold flowers and a delicate scent are a winning combination.

ALSO TRY

Other easy roses for beginners are:
- *Rosa* **Roald Dahl** **('Ausowlish')** produces rich clusters of scented orange blooms all summer and is highly disease-resistant.
- *R.* **Knock Out** **('Radrazz')** is a low, bushy plant that produces semi-double cherry-red flowers in masses.
- *R.* **'The Fairy'** (pictured right) is a Polyantha rose distinguished by sprays of small, pink, double flowers.

***Rosa* For Your Eyes Only ('Cheweyesup')** offers great disease resistance and abundant dark-eyed, single blooms that last well into fall.

FASCINATION

This easy rose bears multitudes of soft pink, cup-shaped flowers in trusses of up to eight blooms through summer and into fall. The blooms open with coral tints and age to a salmon-pink. FASCINATION's bushy habit and easy-going nature make it ideal for a variety of uses—from massed planting in rose gardens and parterres, to growing at the front of borders or in pots on the patio.

CULTIVAR NAME 'Poulmax'
ROSE TYPE Group 1, Floribunda
FLOWERING Repeats through summer and into fall
FLOWER SIZE Around 2¼ in (6 cm) across, held in clusters
FLOWER SCENT Light, sweet perfume
VIGOR Strong
DISEASE RESISTANCE Good
HARDINESS −4°F (−20°C)

FEATURES

Bred in Denmark, this popular plant was named Rose of the Year 1999 by the British Association of Rose Breeders. It is a compact, upright-growing Floribunda rose that reaches heights of around 30 in (75 cm). The plant bears masses of flowers in groups of up to eight at the tops of the stems. The blooms are open and rather cup-shaped, described by some as "camellia-like." They are coral-pink when they first open, aging attractively to a salmon-pink hue. Flowering is wonderfully profuse: prompt deadheading results in further flushes of flowers through the growing season until the first frosts of fall. The foliage is dark green, glossy, and usually free from signs of infection—this is a rose with good disease resistance.

GARDEN USES

This versatile rose has many uses. It needs a sunny, open position but is not fussy about aspect, standing a little shade through the day. It will grow in most moist, but adequately drained, soils. Relatively compact and remarkably floriferous, it has great impact when planted in groups within the low hedge of a parterre or as a flowering hedge itself. FASCINATION is vigorous enough to hold its own among smaller perennials in a mixed border as long as competition is controlled and the plant is not crowded. Its pink flowers look spectacular when grown alongside white or apricot roses, or contrast beautifully with soft blue lavender or *Nepeta*. This rose is also worth trying in a large container.

CARE AND MAINTENANCE

This rose is mostly trouble free and will perform well if you get basic care right. Feed and mulch well in spring before it gets into growth; after flowers have faded, deadhead promptly to ensure rapid repeat displays. Prune in winter as for Group 1 roses (see p.38) .

Dense clusters of cup-shaped blooms make this rose ideal for flowering hedges.

FOR YOUR EYES ONLY

This rose is one of the finest introductions of recent years, and has proved to be easy grow and highly disease-resistant. It offers remarkably profuse displays of five-petaled single flowers from late spring until the frosts. Its blooms, which open apricot and fade to pink, have a distinctive red "eye"; they are open and held in clusters, presenting a tempting target for pollinators.

CULTIVAR NAME 'Cheweyesup'
ROSE TYPE Group 1, modern shrub rose
FLOWERING Repeats through summer and into fall
FLOWER SIZE 2¼–3¼in (6–8cm) across, held in showy clusters
FLOWER SCENT Light citrus perfume
VIGOR Strong
DISEASE RESISTANCE Excellent
HARDINESS Around −4°F (−20°C)

Two-tone flowers give this rose distinctive visual appeal.

FEATURES

This cultivar, which was bred from dark-eyed *Rosa persica* to provide its spectacular coloration, was named Rose of the Year 2015 by the British Association of Rose Breeders. It is single flowered—a form that has recently gained popularity for its natural shape and appeal to pollinating insects. FOR YOUR EYES ONLY has a long season, the first blooms opening in late spring: initially, these are apricot with a red eye, but they fade to pink with age. The plants are bushy and well branched with thorny stems. They reach around 36 in (90cm) in height.

GARDEN USES

This rose is tolerant of light shade and will flower profusely, even in poor soils as long as they are well drained. The single flowers give it a "wild rose" quality, which means that it pairs well with natural-looking perennials, such as grasses, *Digitalis*, and geraniums, and looks at home in gravel gardens beside *Cistus*, *Artemisia,* and *Salvia*. It does well in raised beds and large containers.

CARE AND MAINTENANCE

With excellent disease resistance, this rose is simple to maintain under the usual regime of watering, feeding, and topdressing. Pruning this modern Shrub rose is a little different to the Group 1 method: carry out an initial prune after flowering in late fall to tidy and prevent wind damage, then in late winter cut down by around a third to strong outward-facing buds, thinning out old weak stems in the center. Use gloves; its thorns are vicious.

ALSO TRY

Try these other attractive single-flowered Group 1 roses:
- **R. 'Dainty Bess'** (pictured below) has large, pink, lightly fragrant flowers.
- **R. 'Golden Wings'** is a Shrub rose that freely produces scented large, yellow flowers and decorative hips.
- **R. 'Sally Holmes'** has clusters of primrose-cream single flowers on a large shrub.

GERTRUDE JEKYLL

This much-loved cultivar from UK rose breeder David Austin produces soft pink rosette-shaped flowers in small clusters. The sumptuous appearance of the blooms is matched by their heady perfume. The rose repeat flowers well, is disease-resistant, and will stand a little shade; it thrives in rose gardens, borders, cutting gardens, and even in large pots. It can also be used as a flowering hedge.

CULTIVAR NAME 'Ausbord'
ROSE TYPE Group 1, Shrub rose (English rose)
FLOWERING Repeats through summer
FLOWER SIZE 4¾in (10cm) across, held in small clusters
FLOWER SCENT Powerful old rose perfume
VIGOR Strong
DISEASE RESISTANCE Good
HARDINESS −4°F (−20°C)

The flowers are held on upright, particularly thorny stems.

FEATURES

Lovers of old-fashioned roses adore the classic, beautifully quartered, rich pink double blooms of this English rose. Flowers start early, from the end of spring, and keep coming—profusely through much of summer—imbuing the garden with a rich, fruity perfume. The plant itself reaches 3 ft (1 m) in height and spread, and is well covered with foliage from the ground up.

GARDEN USES

This shrub rose prefers a sunny spot but tolerates part-shade. Its vigor makes it well-suited to mixed borders beside perennials or other roses, but it also looks at home in a cottage garden. Its thorny stems and bushy habit make it a good candidate for a flowering hedge, while the heavily perfumed flowers make it irresistible for cutting and bringing indoors.

CARE AND MAINTENANCE

This is an easy rose that presents growers with few problems. To get the best performance, apply granular feed and mulch in spring and deadhead regularly to promote reflowering through summer. If you grow this rose in a container, top dress with fresh potting mix every two years.

Prune in late summer after flowering, removing dead and diseased growth and cutting most stems back by around a third to maintain its size. Remove a few of the oldest stems each year to encourage young growth.

ALSO TRY

Other English roses to try:
- **R. Eustacia Vye 'Ausegdon'** is a fragrant selection with rosette flowers in a warm, almost glowing pink held on erect stems.
- **R. Harlow Carr ('Aushouse')** (pictured above) is a versatile rose with masses of scented pink flowers all summer long.
- **R. The Lark Ascending ('Ausursula')** has fluttery, glowing apricot-yellow blooms, held in clusters.

GOLDEN CELEBRATION

Few other selections have the floral firepower of this showy English rose, which freely produces glowing, cupped blooms all summer. The blooms are so large that they usually weigh down branches and nod from the stems in appealing fashion. Used in mixed borders, planted in containers, or even enjoyed as a hedge, it offers great value while proving tough and disease-resistant.

CULTIVAR NAME 'Ausgold'
ROSE TYPE Group 1, Shrub rose (English rose)
FLOWERING Repeats through summer
FLOWER SIZE 4¾–5½ in (12–14 cm) across, held in small clusters
FLOWER SCENT Strong Tea rose perfume
VIGOR Strong
DISEASE RESISTANCE Good
HARDINESS Around −4°F (−20°C)

FEATURES

This spectacular English rose from David Austin was introduced in 1992. Its golden-yellow double flowers open from red-tinged buds, becoming large and showy as they mature. The cup-shaped blooms, which are held in small clusters, have a strong, fruity, Tea rose scent and attract bees and other pollinating insects. The display starts in late spring and lasts well into fall. The plants are vigorous, well-branched, and leafy from the base, growing into dome-shaped shrubs around 4 ft (1.2 m) tall.

GARDEN USES

Like many other English roses, this is a versatile plant, thriving in a range of situations. It will tolerate a little shade but is best kept clear of overhanging branches. GOLDEN CELEBRATION is vigorous and tall and so rises above shorter competition in a mixed border. It is most impressive in more formal situations, such as in a parterre or a raised bed on a terrace, but still works in a cottage garden. Given enough space, the tall flower-laden branches will fall into gentle arches. These roses are sturdy enough to grow in large containers where they create a superb focal point They also make great flowering hedges and good standards.

CARE AND MAINTENANCE

Despite its large and impressive flowers, this is an easy rose to keep. All that flower power needs feeding: add granular fertilizer and mulch plants in spring. Maintain deadheading and more flowers will develop. Pruning follows other Group 1 roses, with a few tweaks. Once established, cut stems back in winter by around a third; trim by less if you want it to grow taller.

Flower heads nod appealingly from tall branches.

HOT CHOCOLATE

The dramatic pinkish-red-brown blooms of this highly recommended modern Floribunda rose have proved a hit with many gardeners. The sweetly fragrant, cup-shaped, ruffled double flowers are produced in large trusses all summer. The plant is typically vigorous and bushy, with super-shiny dark green leaves that glisten with good health, providing visual contrast with the lush blooms.

CULTIVAR NAME 'Wekpaltlez'
ROSE TYPE Group 1, Floribunda
FLOWERING Repeats through summer and into fall
FLOWER SIZE 2¾–3¼ in (7–8 cm) across, held in clusters
FLOWER SCENT Powerful sweet fruity perfume
VIGOR Strong
DISEASE RESISTANCE Excellent
HARDINESS −4°F (−20°C)

FEATURES

This distinctive US-bred rose was named Rose of the Year 2006 by the British Association of Rose Breeders. Its flowers are highly unusual in color, their tone altering as they age. Young blooms are coppery-orange but then develop brick-red or pinkish tints that may appear russet brown in shifting light. The blooms are cupped and open-centered, of ruffled appearance, and sweetly fragrant; they are held in generous heads. Deadheading results in further flushes of flowers through summer and well into fall.

The plant itself is bushy and reaches heights of around 3 ft (1 m). The stems are particularly thorny and support superbly shiny foliage that sets off the flowers beautifully.

GARDEN USES

Thanks to its tough constitution, Hot Chocolate can be used in a variety of ways. It makes a bold choice for a dedicated rose border, group planting suits it well, and its bushy nature means it can be grown as a flowering hedge. It is less well suited to mixed borders: a better bet is a large container—this way, you can enjoy the unusual flowers and sweet scent close to the house. This rose can also be trained as a standard, in which form its flowers are elevated close to nose height.

CARE AND MAINTENANCE

This is an easy rose that usually needs only annual feeding with granular fertilizer and manure mulch in spring. Prune this bushy, twiggy plant after flowering to tidy; then in late winter cut back by around a third to strong outward-facing buds, thinning old weak stems from the center.

Russet-brown flowers mark this rose out as special.

ALSO TRY

Other brown-tinted roses include:
- **R. Belle Epoque ('Fryyaboo')** (pictured right) has large flowers that are peach colored within a bronze outside.
- **R. 'Julia's Rose'** is a large-flowered shrub rose with lightly scented coppery-buff blooms, high centered at first, then cupped.
- **R. Mokarosa ('Frywitty')** has fragrant, crème-caramel tinted blooms.

INDIAN SUMMER

This low-growing, rather leafy plant has become deservedly popular with gardeners since its introduction in 1991. Everything about this rose says elegance; its large high-centered blooms are shapely in bud and in full flower. Warm, creamy apricot in color, they have a sweet pea perfume. The flowers retain their color well throughout the season and are not easily damaged by rain.

CULTIVAR NAME 'Peaperfume'
ROSE TYPE Group 1, Hybrid Tea
FLOWERING Repeats through summer
FLOWER SIZE 3¼–4 in (8–10 cm) across, held singly
FLOWER SCENT Superb sweet perfume
VIGOR Average
DISEASE RESISTANCE Fair
HARDINESS −4°F (−20°C)

FEATURES

INDIAN SUMMER is a fine garden rose, admired for its double flowers, which are peachy yellow with slightly darker, more apricot reverses. Each bloom is initially high centered before becoming looser and more cup shaped. Flowers are freely produced through summer and have a powerful and wonderfully sweet scent. The plants themselves are compact, reaching around 25 in (65 cm) in height, and the stems are stout and stiff, with quite lush glossy green foliage.

GARDEN USES

Grow this rose in a sunny, open position, and avoid planting it below overhanging vegetation because it does not like competition. With its low, compact stature it is well suited for planting at the front of a border, but make sure it has plenty of space. Group planting suits it well: try it in a dedicated rose border, parterre, island bed, or even at the foot of a garden sculpture—it will flower well through the summer so it is good for highlighting a focal point.

With its heady fragrance, INDIAN SUMMER is well-suited for growing close to the house and, being a small and stocky plant, it adapts well to life in a pot. This rose is also one to consider for growing as a cut flower.

This free-flowering, beautifully scented cultivar has become a garden favorite.

CARE AND MAINTENANCE

This classic cultivar has reasonable disease resistance but can suffer from blackspot (see p.44) when stressed, such as in hot, dry spells. If it is affected, pick off all affected foliage and clear fallen petals and foliage from below. You may need to apply a fungicide spray in a bad year. Prune plants in winter as per other Group 1 roses; being compact-growing, it will not need much more than a tidy.

IVOR'S ROSE

Introduced in 2004 by UK rose breeder Amanda Beales, this modern shrub rose has proven to be highly disease-resistant, impressively tolerant of summer heat, and wonderfully long flowering, with a season that lasts well into fall. It produces generous clusters of sumptuous rosette-form red-pink double flowers held above healthy, glossy, purple-flushed foliage.

CULTIVAR NAME 'Beadonald'
ROSE TYPE Group 1, Shrub rose
FLOWERING Repeats through summer and into fall
FLOWER SIZE 4 in (10 cm) across, held in clusters
FLOWER SCENT Little
VIGOR Strong
DISEASE RESISTANCE Excellent
HARDINESS Around −4°F (−20°C)

This generous rose produces richly colored fully double flowers.

FEATURES

The red-pink double flowers of this popular cultivar take the form of a tight rosette, rather in the style of an old-fashioned rose. They open from richly tinted buds and are held on tall, slender, maroon-red stems. The blooms are produced in great profusion all summer and continue well into fall.

Plants can reach a height of 4 ft (1.2 m) and are bushy in habit, remaining leafy down to ground level. The foliage is red-tinted when young and becomes a lush, glossy, dark green, retaining its appearance even through hot, dry spells of weather and also well into mild winters.

GARDEN USES

This is a versatile rose. Its old-fashioned flowers suit a cottage garden, but work equally well in more modern or formal areas, especially when planted in a group. A long flowering period makes it suited to high-profile positions where it will be seen often—for example, next to a door or window. With its leafy, bushy habit it needs no companions to mask bare lower stems and it also performs well in containers.

CARE AND MAINTENANCE

Get this rose into healthy growth in spring with a good annual feed using granular fertilizer and then a mulch of manure or garden compost. Keep plants deadheaded to ensure consistent reflowering through the season. If grown in a pot, top dress with fresh potting mix every couple of years. This is a modern Shrub rose and has slightly different pruning needs to other Group 1 roses. Lightly prune after flowering has finished: in late winter, cut stems back by about one third to strong outward-facing buds, thinning out old, weak stems and any signs of disease or damage.

JACQUELINE DU PRÉ

This modern Shrub rose has blush-white semi-double flowers that open unusually early in spring. The open-hearted blooms are distinctive, presenting a prominent crown of gold-tipped, red stamens that stand out well from the petals. The vigorous nature of this cultivar means that it integrates well with other planting, making it an asset to any garden.

CULTIVAR NAME 'Harwanna'
ROSE TYPE Group 1, modern Shrub rose
FLOWERING Repeats from spring well into summer
FLOWER SIZE 3¼–4 in (8–10 cm) across, held in clusters
FLOWER SCENT Lemony-musk perfume
VIGOR Strong
DISEASE RESISTANCE Good
HARDINESS Around −4°F (−20°C)

FEATURES

Introduced in 1985, JACQUELINE DU PRÉ is among the most glamorous of roses, and one of the first to flower in the spring garden. The blooms open from pink buds and the petals initially have a warm pink tint before turning pure white, contrasting with the distinctive red stamens at the center. The semi-double flowers are held in clusters. As with most other modern Shrub roses, JACQUELINE DU PRÉ is bushy in form with dark green leaves down to the ground. It grows to a height of around 3 ft (1 m).

GARDEN USES

JACQUELINE DU PRÉ deserves a place in a dedicated rose border but grows well with other plants in a mixed planting. If you have a predominantly white garden, this cultivar is highly recommended because its blush flowers will add a hint of warmth to the plain palette. This rose will bring the feel of high summer to a spring garden, so deserves a place in full sun; it will repeat well so you can rely on it all summer if you deadhead. Its bushy nature means it may also be worth considering for container cultivation.

CARE AND MAINTENANCE

This is an easy rose; apply a dose of granular rose feed and add a manure mulch around the base in spring to get it off to a good start. Watch for diseases in summer and remove any affected material. Pruning of this modern Shrub rose is a little different to that of other Group 1 members. Carry out an initial prune after flowering in late fall to tidy, then in late winter cut back by around a third to strong outward-facing buds, thinning out old, weak stems.

The open-centered flowers feature beautiful contrasting red stamens.

ALSO TRY

Other modern Shrub roses for white gardens include:
- **R. 'Little White Pet'** is a dwarf rose that gives a dense display of small pompom blooms all summer long.
- **R. MACMILLAN NURSE ('Beamac')** (pictured above) holds its creamy-white rosette-shaped, double flowers in clusters.
- **R. PEARL DRIFT ('Leggab')** is a sprawling shrub rose with large, sweetly fragranced flowers that are white with a tinge of pink.

'JUST JOEY'

Derived from the classic, highly scented FRAGRANT CLOUD ('Tanellis'), this impressive Hybrid Tea rose has many admirers due to its large, sweetly fragrant, soft orange blooms. These develop from shapely buds, high-centered on opening, but becoming ruffled and cup-shaped as the flowers age. This is a rose that deserves and repays a little extra care and attention.

CULTIVAR NAME 'Just Joey'
ROSE TYPE Group 1, Hybrid Tea
FLOWERING Repeats through summer and into fall
FLOWER SIZE 4¾–5½ in (12-14 cm) across, held singly
FLOWER SCENT Strong and sweetly fragrant
VIGOR Average
DISEASE RESISTANCE Tolerable
HARDINESS −4°F (−20°C)

FEATURES

This rose remains hugely popular with gardeners despite having been introduced as long ago as 1973. Its impressive warm coppery-orange flowers are large and perfectly shaped, fading from orange to coppery buff. They open singly or sometimes in small groups from elegant red-veined buds. 'Just Joey' reflowers through to mid-fall if it is regularly deadheaded and the weather is mild. This bushy shrub has an open spreading habit and reaches a height of around 3 ft (1 m). Its foliage is copper-tinged when young, becoming medium green with maturity.

GARDEN USES

'Just Joey' thrives in sunny locations but can tolerate a little shade during the day. It is at its best in a dedicated rose border, although it will grow at the front of a mixed bed as long as you control neighboring plants. It looks superb when planted in groups within a low hedge-edged parterre or island bed and can also be trained into a standard to bring its sweetly scented flowers to nose height. Alternatively, grow it in the cutting garden—the flowers look great in a bud vase.

Highly fragrant orange flowers pop out from dark coppery-green foliage.

CARE AND MAINTENANCE

Disease resistance is good for a rose of this age, but worse than that of modern cultivars. Be sure to give 'Just Joey' the best start in spring by feeding it well with granular fertilizer and applying a mulch of well-rotted manure. Water regularly in the summer and do not let the plant get stressed by heat or drought. Clear fallen leaves and petals that may harbor pests and diseases and apply fungicide if needed. Prune as other Group 1 cultivars (see p.38).

LADY OF SHALOTT

This vigorous Shrub rose is great value because it provides color in the garden from early summer until the first frosts. It produces masses of large, fragrant, glowing orange double flowers that open from red-tinged buds. It is an extremely versatile selection, growing well in full sun but also tolerating light shade. It can even be trained as a climber or grow in a large container.

CULTIVAR NAME 'Ausnyson'

ROSE TYPE Group 1, Shrub rose (English rose)

FLOWERING Repeats through summer into fall

FLOWER SIZE Up to 4in (10cm) across, held in clusters

FLOWER SCENT Distinct Tea rose scent

VIGOR Strong, can be trained as a small climber

DISEASE RESISTANCE Excellent

HARDINESS −4°F (−20°C)

FEATURES

One of the finest English roses from breeder David Austin, LADY OF SHALOTT was introduced in 2009. The flowers are superb; large and fully double, they appear in clusters, opening rich coppery-orange from red-tinged buds. They soften in tone as they age, the petals developing golden and pinkish tints. Flowers have a spiced Tea Rose scent and are held at the ends of slightly arching branches. The show starts in early summer and the blooms are continually produced well into fall, when the last flowers echo the fiery colors of falling leaves. The plants are well-branched from the base and bushy, forming a dome-shaped shrub.

GARDEN USES

This rose is simple to accommodate in the garden, performing well in part shade so long as it gets some sun through the day. It is vigorous enough for a mixed border alongside perennials or other roses; alternatively, planted by a sunny sheltered wall or fence, it can be trained as a small but impressive climber. Grown in this way, it can reach 10ft (3m). LADY OF SHALOTT also performs exceptionally well in large containers, forming a rounded plant with arching stems cascading with flowers. It makes a good standard rose.

This shrub rose carries masses of glowing blooms that have a spicy scent.

CARE AND MAINTENANCE

This is a robust rose that needs little more than spring feeding and mulching. Pruning follows that of other Group 1 roses. Once established, cut the plant's stems back by around one third to maintain size; trim by less if you want it to grow taller. Always remove dead and diseased growth and retained foliage.

LOVESTRUCK

Red-flowered roses are always popular and this award-winning modern floribunda pairs impressive, showy heads of sumptuous double cherry-red blooms with strong disease resistance. Healthy, glossy foliage and a compact habit help make this a great rose for a dedicated border or even for mixed planting. The plant will flower well into fall if deadheaded regularly.

CULTIVAR NAME 'Dicommatac'
ROSE TYPE Group 1, Floribunda
FLOWERING Repeats through summer and into fall
FLOWER SIZE 4 in (10 cm) across, held in large clusters
FLOWER SCENT Light perfume
VIGOR Average
DISEASE RESISTANCE Excellent
HARDINESS −4°F (−20°C)

A tidy habit and months of dependable color make this a good container rose.

FEATURES

Named Rose of the Year 2018 by the British Association of Rose Breeders, LOVESTRUCK is a great choice if you are looking for a classic red-flowered cultivar. The mildly scented blooms are usually held in large, showy clusters of 18–20 individual flowers atop upright stems. When the blooms open from dark red buds they are initially high-centered and cherry-red in color, with an appealing swirl of petals. As they age, flowers become more cupped and their outer petals develop rich purple tints. The plants are compact, growing to heights of around 3 ft (1 m), making them well suited to massed planting. Regular deadheading results in a display that lasts into fall.

GARDEN USES

LOVESTRUCK looks great when planted en masse in a dedicated rose border, and its compact size and long flowering season make it a favorite for formal use in a bed or edged with box hedging. Alternatively, try a group of three plants within a hot-color-themed border to inject some reliable flower power; this rose is tough and will stand a little competition. Grow it in reasonably fertile soil in an open, sunny position.

CARE AND MAINTENANCE

A dose of granular fertilizer and application of mulch in spring will power this rose through the year. Keep flower clusters in good condition by removing individual faded blooms, then, once the whole head has finished, cut it down; more flowering stems will soon arise. Watch out for aphids and disease (see pp.44–45), especially during hot, wet, or unseasonably cool weather. Prune as all other Group 1 roses (see p.38).

MARGARET MERRIL

This much-loved vintage Floribunda rose is quite irresistible for its delicious scent and its elegant ivory-white, double blooms that almost seem to glow in the garden at twilight. It repeats well if plants are deadheaded regularly, allowing you to enjoy its scent into fall. That delectable fragrance makes this cultivar a popular choice for the cutting garden.

CULTIVAR NAME 'Harkuly'
ROSE TYPE Group 1, Floribunda
FLOWERING Repeats through summer and into fall
FLOWER SIZE 3¼ in (8 cm) across, held in clusters
FLOWER SCENT Superb powerful perfume
VIGOR Average
DISEASE RESISTANCE Tolerable
HARDINESS −4°F (−20°C)

FEATURES

Introduced in 1977 by Harkness, this cultivar is considered to be one of the most highly scented of all roses, with a fragrance described as rich and sweet with a hint of lemon. The visual appeal of the flowers follows close behind their fragrance: blooms emerge high-centered, colored ivory-white with a shimmer of pink especially at the heart of the flower. As the flowers age, they become more cup-shaped and open, with a boss of golden stamens. The plant itself is rather upright, growing to around 3 ft (1 m) high: if deadheaded regularly it will repeat in flushes throughout the summer.

Cooler weather tends to favor more pinkish color in the blooms.

GARDEN USES

This rose works well when planted in groups in a dedicated border or island bed, perhaps around a central feature, such as an urn or sculpture. MARGARET MERRIL will tolerate life in a mixed border if the competition is not too fierce: it looks stunning alongside silver-leaved and other white flowered companions. Try it in a large container on the terrace—it likes a sunny site but is fairly robust and not too fussy. It also makes a good standard.

CARE AND MAINTENANCE

This rose is susceptible to blackspot (see p.44): the best way to prevent this fungal disease is to avoid putting plants under stress. Start by feeding well in spring with a granular fertilizer and add a decent mulch of manure. Then keep a sharp eye out for aphids and disease, and clear any organic debris from around the plants; water well in dry weather. In a bad year you might need to spray with fungicide. Prune as other Group 1 cultivars.

ALSO TRY

These white or cream Group 1 roses also have a good scent:

- *R. POLAR STAR* ('Tanlarpost') is a Hybrid Tea rose with large, creamy-white, high-centered blooms.
- *R. 'White Wings'* features charming large, pure white single flowers with contrasting dark stamens that open from long pointed buds.
- *R. PASCALI* ('Lenip') (pictured above) has elegant, lightly scented cream-white blooms on a vigorous, free-flowering plant.

'MRS. OAKLEY FISHER'

This single-flowered old rose has enduring appeal. Its orange-yellow blooms have a delicate beauty and appear in profusion through summer, reaching a peak late in the year when cooler conditions seem to boost its performance until the first hard frosts arrive. The fluttering flowers blend perfectly with autumnal richness, while in spring the foliage is richly red-tinted.

CULTIVAR NAME 'Mrs. Oakley Fisher'
ROSE TYPE Group 1, Hybrid Tea
FLOWERING Repeats through summer and into fall
FLOWER SIZE 4–4¾ in (10–12 cm) across, held singly or in small groups
FLOWER SCENT Sweet fruity perfume
VIGOR Strong
DISEASE RESISTANCE Good
HARDINESS –4°F (–20°C)

FEATURES

This Hybrid Tea rose possesses the simple beauty of a wild rose but the color, repeat flowering, and refinement of a great garden plant. Introduced in 1921 by Cant, it has remained a favorite for over a century. Its single flowers open from red-tinged buds, becoming quite large when fully open. They are a glowing soft apricot with contrasting reddish stamens and a sweet, fruity perfume. Growing up to 4 ft (1.2 m), bushes are vigorous with slender red stems and dark green foliage.

GARDEN USES

'Mrs. Oakley Fisher' integrates well into many gardens: it tolerates a little competition, and its flowers blend into almost any color scheme. Early in the year this rose looks stunning underplanted with green *Alchemilla mollis*; later in the season it works well alongside lilac and pale blue asters, or with sky-blue *Salvia uliginosa* or purple *Verbena bonariensis*—these slender-flowered perennials not offering much competition to trouble the rose. Individual flowers are pretty when used in small arrangements, making this a good rose for the cutting garden.

This well-scented rose has delicate single flowers, and is easy to grow.

CARE AND MAINTENANCE

An easy, tolerant garden rose, 'Mrs. Oakley Fisher' responds well to the application of granular rose feed and a manure mulch in spring. Deadhead regularly for repeat displays in flushes until the first frosts. Plants are quite resistant to disease for a selection of this age but look out for aphids and blackspot (*see pp.44–45*). Prune as for any other Group 1 rose (*see p.38*).

PEACE

Raised in 1935 by French rosarian Francis Meilland, PEACE became probably the best-known rose in the world when its name was announced on the day Berlin fell at the end of World War II. Millions have been planted and it remains a much-loved and superlative selection to this day, featuring huge well-scented, cupped double flowers of pink-tinged, primrose-yellow.

CULTIVAR NAME 'Madame A. Meilland'
ROSE TYPE Group 1, Hybrid Tea
FLOWERING Repeats through summer and into fall
FLOWER SIZE Around 6in (15cm) across, held singly
FLOWER SCENT Strong sweet perfume
VIGOR Strong
DISEASE RESISTANCE Fair
HARDINESS −4°F (−20°C)

FEATURES

Regarded by some experts as among the finest of all Hybrid Tea roses and once voted the world's favorite rose, PEACE became a symbolic plant for those who had lived through World War II. Its flowers are superb, developing from red-tinged yellow buds that open initially into high-centered flowers of classic form. As they mature, they open out into huge rounded, cup-shaped blooms. The petals are soft primrose-yellow, edged with pink tints, and have a beautiful sweet, fruity perfume. This rose has large, glossy leaves and is vigorous, reaching a height of 5ft (1.5m).

GARDEN USES

PEACE needs plenty of space to grow and in which to display its huge flowers; however, it is not fussy about site, tolerating a little shade. You can use it in borders, where it is happy with other roses, and can be underplanted with small spring bulbs or low-growing perennials such as *Geranium sanguineum*. It might also do well on the corner of a mixed border, as long as it has plenty of space. Its spectacular flowers make it a most desirable rose for cutting gardens—the blooms are best displayed singly in a bud vase. It is sometimes grown as a standard.

Peace is widely grown for its huge, beautifully perfumed flowers.

CARE AND MAINTENANCE

PEACE can be susceptible to blackspot, rust, and mildew (see p.44) so avoid stressing plants in summer. Give them a good start in spring by applying granular fertilizer and a decent mulch of manure. Pick off any affected foliage and keep the area around the plant clear of any debris. You may need to apply a fungicide spray in a bad year. In dry, hot weather, water well to keep the plant growing strongly. Deadhead regularly and you will enjoy further flower flushes, well into fall. Prune as other Group 1 cultivars (see p.38).

PURPLE TIGER

Producing small clusters of scented flowers that are strikingly marbled in purple and pink, this rose is a great choice for gardeners who like to try something a bit different. It reblooms well and has a tidy, compact form, with slender stems that are almost thornless. The flowers look as good in a vase as they do in the border—and they have a surprisingly good fragrance.

CULTIVAR NAME 'Jacpurr'
ROSE TYPE Group 1, Floribunda
FLOWERING Repeats through summer
FLOWER SIZE 3¼–4 in (8–10 cm) across, held in clusters
FLOWER SCENT Strong, sweet perfume
VIGOR Average
DISEASE RESISTANCE Fair
HARDINESS Around 5°F (−15°C)

The striped and marbled flowers are held in small clusters.

FEATURES

Introduced in 1991 from the US where it was bred by Jack Christensen, PURPLE TIGER is an unusual rose. The flowers open as high-centered blooms, striped or marbled in purple on a pink background with flecks of white.

They become softer in hue with age but also rather variable depending on weather conditions—no two blooms are quite alike. The plant is relatively compact, reaching a height of around 30 in (75 cm): its mid-green foliage is held on almost thorn-free stems. Plants repeat bloom well through summer if deadheaded. This is a good choice for gardeners with a little experience who want to try something different.

GARDEN USES

This rose needs a sunny spot in well-drained, fertile soil. Plant it where its fascinating flowers are elevated toward eye level—a raised bed on a terrace or patio is ideal, but a tall, wide container will do the job. Otherwise, try planting a small group in a rose garden, at the corner of a border, or in an island bed; nearby silvery planting will complement the flowers without distracting from their beauty, but avoid too much competition. PURPLE TIGER is also a good choice for a cutting border.

CARE AND MAINTENANCE

This is not a difficult rose to grow, but it requires a little care and vigilance to avoid blackspot (see p.44), especially in hot, dry years. Start the growing season by feeding with a granular fertilizer and mulch. Make sure the rose is well watered throughout the summer and remove any diseased foliage promptly. Be prepared to spray with fungicide if blackspot persists. Keep on top of deadheading and good plant hygiene, and top-dress annually if you are growing this rose in a pot. Prune as for other Group 1 roses (see p.38).

RHAPSODY IN BLUE

With sweetly scented clusters of semi-double flowers that have purple-blue petals and golden stamens, this modern shrub rose attracts plenty of attention from gardeners and pollinating insects alike. Tall, upright-growing, and disease resistant, it integrates well into mixed plantings where the unusual hue of its flowers provides exciting new color associations to explore.

CULTIVAR NAME 'Frantasia'
ROSE TYPE Group 1, Shrub rose
FLOWERING Repeats through summer
FLOWER SIZE 2¼–2¾ in (6–7 cm) across, held in clusters
FLOWER SCENT Rich sweet perfume
VIGOR Strong
DISEASE RESISTANCE Good
HARDINESS −4°F (−20°C)

FEATURES

Introduced by UK rose breeder Frank Cowlishaw, RHAPSODY IN BLUE created a stir in the gardening world with its unusual flower color; it was later named Rose of the Year 2003 by the British Association of Rose Breeders. The blooms are modestly sized but create an imposing effect because they are carried in generous, sweetly fragrant clusters, which attract many pollinator species. On opening, the semi-double flowers are shapely and a rich purple-mauve color, but they soon open out and become more cupped, with prominent golden stamens at their center. As they age, the flowers become more gray-purple with a blue tinge.

The plant itself is tough, vigorous, and disease resistant. Its upright thorny stems can reach a height of around 4 ft (1.2 m) in a good year.

GARDEN USES

With its unusual flower color, this is a rose that cries out for use in a mixed border. Happily, its tough constitution and tall-growing bushy habit make this possible. Try growing it alongside the shimmering silver leaves of plants such as *Melianthus major*, or set up an impressive contrast to its deep purplish color with orange lupins or lilies.

Ensure that it gets plenty of sun—this is not a plant for the shade—and avoid planting it too tightly because it doesn't like competition. Alternatively, group several plants in a rose garden for a spectacular splash of color—this looks good with low hedging around it to mask the rather tall stems. This rose will also grow well as a standard.

CARE AND MAINTENANCE

In general, treat and feed this as other Group I roses. This is a modern Shrub rose, so carry out an initial prune after flowering in late fall to tidy, then in late winter cut down by around a third to strong outward-facing buds, thinning out old, weak stems.

With strident purple, semi-double flowers, this rose never fails to grab attention.

SCARBOROUGH FAIR

With semi-double, musk-scented flowers of soft pink held in generous sprays, this rose is packed with discreet charm. It is a tough, almost problem-free plant that is equally at home in a mixed border, rose garden, or container, and can even be grown successfully as a hedge. It will attract pollinating insects and has decorative fall hips to prolong its appeal.

CULTIVAR NAME 'Ausoran'
ROSE TYPE Group 1, Shrub rose (English rose)
FLOWERING Repeats through summer and into fall
FLOWER SIZE 2¼–2¾ in (6–7 cm) across, held in sprays
FLOWER SCENT Musky, old rose perfume
VIGOR Good
DISEASE RESISTANCE Excellent
HARDINESS −4°F (−20°C)

FEATURES

This charming but understated cultivar is one of breeder David Austin's English roses. It bears its modestly sized flowers in generous clusters to make an impressive display. The semi-double pale pink blooms quickly become cupped, displaying a central boss of golden stamens that is a magnet to pollinators. The flowers have a musky scent; after they fade, if you do not deadhead, showy orange hips develop in clusters at branch tips, giving the garden color until late winter. This tough rose will reach heights of around 3 ft (1 m).

GARDEN USES

SCARBOROUGH FAIR integrates well into mixed borders as long as it has enough space; it will stand most soils provided they are not waterlogged. It prefers a sunny location but will tolerate some shade, succeeding even by a north wall as long as the site is open. The flower color is sympathetic to various plantings; try it alongside silver companions such as artemisia or other soft pink blooms. Plant en masse to fill an area with color, or try growing this rose as a flowering hedge.

CARE AND MAINTENANCE

This cultivar responds well to annual spring feeding. Deadheading ensures continuity of flowering, but if you leave the last heads you'll get a show of hips. Pruning follows other Group 1 roses but with a few tweaks. Once established, cut stems back by around a third to maintain size, trim by less if you want it to grow taller. Remove dead and diseased growth and any retained foliage.

Like most other English roses, SCARBOROUGH FAIR does well in containers.

ALSO TRY

Beneficial insects will not only pollinate your roses but help reduce pest populations. Try the roses below to help attract more of these beasts into your garden:
- *R. 'Francis E. Lester'* (pictured right) is a rambler with white and pink single flowers in early summer. It produces great orange hips.
- *R. KEW GARDENS* ('Ausfence') yields masses of insect-friendly single white flowers all summer long.

SIMPLY THE BEST

This award-winning rose is prized for its sweetly scented, large double flowers. These beautifully formed blooms are a dazzling shade of burnt coppery orange, fading gradually to apricot-yellow, and stand out well against the plant's glossy green foliage. SIMPLY THE BEST is a perfect selection for group planting in a rose border, or adding to the cutting garden.

CULTIVAR NAME 'Macamster'
ROSE TYPE Group I, Hybrid Tea
FLOWERING Repeats through summer and into fall
FLOWER SIZE 4 in (10 cm) across, usually held singly
FLOWER SCENT Sweet perfume
VIGOR Strong
DISEASE RESISTANCE Good
HARDINESS −4°F (−20°C)

FEATURES

Bred by Sam McGredy in the US, this was named Rose of the Year 2002 by the British Association of Rose Growers. SIMPLY THE BEST is a treat in the garden throughout the summer and is tough, vigorous, and easy to maintain, with good disease resistance.

Its double flowers open in a rich, almost burnt orange color before developing more muted apricot tones as they age. They seem to glow against the dark green glossy foliage and have a sweet scent, too—all characteristics that make this cultivar a great choice for cutting. It will repeat flower in flushes if deadheaded. This is a somewhat bushy plant that will reach a height of around 4 ft (1.2 m) in good growing conditions.

GARDEN USES

SIMPLY THE BEST likes an open site in full sun and demands a fertile, well-drained soil. It is ideally suited to a traditional rose garden or planted in a group within an island bed. It blends perfectly with yellow roses and contrasts to great effect with purple-tinted selections, such as RHAPSODY IN BLUE. You could try it on the corner of a mixed border as long as there is sufficient space around it—this is not a rose that enjoys a lot of competition.

This rose usually produces one flower per stem—ideal for cutting.

CARE AND MAINTENANCE

Treat as you would any other Hybrid Tea rose; apply granular plant food in spring and mulch with well-rotted manure or garden compost to get it growing strongly from the start. Watch for aphids and disease (see pp.44–45) through summer; it is pretty disease-resistant so long as growing conditions remain good. Prune in winter as for any Group I rose (see p.38).

Rosa **SCARBOROUGH FAIR** is hard to beat for sheer profusion of flowers. Delicate soft pink blooms belie this cultivar's robust nature.

TWICE IN A BLUE MOON

The sophisticated lilac-blue hue of this rose, paired with its powerful fruity scent, makes it virtually irresistible. It has huge and magnificently shaped flowers that repeat well—keep deadheading, and you'll enjoy these glorious blooms well into the fall. This is an easy-to-grow, spectacular, disease-resistant garden rose that is ideal for both borders and cutting gardens.

CULTIVAR NAME 'Tan96138'
ROSE TYPE Group 1, Hybrid Tea
FLOWERING Repeats through summer and into fall
FLOWER SIZE 4¾–6 in (12–15 cm) across, held singly or in small clusters
FLOWER SCENT Powerful fruity perfume
VIGOR Strong
DISEASE RESISTANCE Good
HARDINESS −4°F (−20°C)

FEATURES

Introduced by German breeders Tantau in 2004, TWICE IN A BLUE MOON has large double blooms that open from purplish buds to form shapely, high-centered flowers. Its silvery-lilac petals are arranged in a perfect swirl. Initially, the flowers develop individually, but later in clusters, and become more cupped with age; they are held on sturdy, almost thornless stems. The dark green foliage is tinged red when young. Plants reach around 4 ft (1.2 m).

This standout cultivar offers good disease resistance and is strong and easy to grow.

GARDEN USES

Planted in sunny borders or rose gardens, TWICE IN A BLUE MOON is a striking rose. Upright in habit, it tolerates some underplanting—initially, with spring bulbs, later with herbaceous plants such as *Agastache*, *Alchemilla*, silvery *Artemisia*, lower-growing *Geranium*, and *Nepeta*. It is often sold as a standard, which helpfully brings the flowers to nose height. Plant it in cutting beds for bringing into the house. Held on long stems, the blooms are terrific for vases and also look superb in a bowl with pink roses—their blue hue seems stronger in this company.

CARE AND MAINTENANCE

In spring, apply a good food, adding a handful of granular fertilizer to the soil above the roots and then a mulch of manure or garden compost over the top, removing any old, fallen rose leaves. Keep watch for aphids as the weather warms, rubbing off any that appear. In summer, inspect for blackspot, rust, or mildew (see p.44), resolving any problems as they arise and keeping the plant clear of fallen debris. This rose is quite sturdy so any problems should be minor. Keep on deadheading, and you'll enjoy the flowers of TWICE IN A BLUE MOON well into the fall. Prune as for other Group 1 roses (see p.38).

YOU'RE BEAUTIFUL

With its glowing pink flowers clustered above sturdy, upright stems, this superb rose makes a big impression. It produces a profusion of double, sugar-pink blooms held in showy clusters all through summer and fall. YOU'RE BEAUTIFUL is also impressively disease resistant, with glossy, healthy foliage and compact, tidy growth that makes it wonderfully simple to manage.

CULTIVAR NAME 'Fryracy'
ROSE TYPE Group 1, Floribunda
FLOWERING Repeats through summer and into fall
FLOWER SIZE 4 in (10 cm) across, held in clusters
FLOWER SCENT Light perfume
VIGOR Strong
DISEASE RESISTANCE Excellent
HARDINESS −4°F (−20°C)

If you admire pink-bloomed roses, YOU'RE BEAUTIFUL is a winner.

FEATURES

YOU'RE BEAUTIFUL was introduced by UK rose breeder Gareth Fryer and named Rose of the Year 2013 by the British Association of Rose Growers. The flowers of this irresistible cultivar open from pink buds held on reddish stems that are generously produced. These striking blooms appear over a long period from around midsummer in unusually large, showy trusses and have a mild, sweet scent. On opening, flowers have a classic high-centered shape, but gradually become more open and cup-shaped with age. At first an even shade of pink, the outer petals eventually fade to almost white. Plants have a neat, bushy habit and reach to around 35 in (90 cm) in height. The mid-green foliage remains notably clean and glossy throughout the season.

GARDEN USES

Thriving in sun but tolerating some shade, this rose, with its neat habit, is ideal for planting in groups in dedicated rose beds. It does well in a small boxwood hedge-edged parterre or grouped in an island bed. It is at its best with others of its own kind, rather than in a mixed border, but you can plant low spring bulbs such as *Crocus* and *Muscari* at its feet. It flourishes in a large pot and can be grown as a standard.

CARE AND MAINTENANCE

This is an easy rose, but it likes a good annual feed with granular fertilizer and mulch at the start of the season. If in a pot, water and feed regularly, and top dress with fresh potting mix every two years. Remove faded blooms from the clusters; once the whole head has faded, cut off for more clusters into fall. Keep the plant healthy, and disease problems are unlikely. Prune as for other Group 1 roses (see p.38).

This repeat-flowering rose is stunning planted in groups in a dedicated bed.

Among the most versatile of the small bush roses, *R.* 'Ballerina' thrives in sun or part shade producing multitudes of charming pollinator-attracting single flowers; it makes a great standard, too.

GROUP 2:
SMALL BUSH ROSES

If you have a small garden, or like to grow your roses in pots or even window boxes, take a close look at the plants in this group. They are highly compact and many have been purposely developed for life in containers. Most will repeat flower very well through the summer and need little in the way of pruning. Some can also be suitable for mass planting in raised beds, while the very tiniest may be used in tabletop planters.

'BALLERINA'

This generously free-flowering plant is vigorous, disease resistant, and more tolerant of shade and poor soil than most roses. It requires remarkably little attention to produce masses of large, showy heads of white and pink single flowers through summer into fall and is generally regarded as an easy plant, particularly well-suited to novice rose growers.

CULTIVAR NAME 'Ballerina'
ROSE TYPE Group 2, Polyantha/Shrub rose
FLOWERING Repeats through summer and into fall
FLOWER SIZE Around 2 in (5 cm) across, held in profuse clusters
FLOWER SCENT Minimal fragrance
VIGOR Strong
DISEASE RESISTANCE Good
HARDINESS Around −4°F (−20°C)

FEATURES

It is hard to find a more tolerant, easy-to-grow, and rewarding rose than 'Ballerina'. Raised in 1937 by UK rose breeder Ann Bentall, it produces huge conical inflorescences of small, white-centered, single flowers. The red petal edges fade to pink with age.

'Ballerina' bears small flowers that resemble apple blossoms.

Deadheading results in repeated blooms; the plant can remain in flower for months. This vigorous rose reaches 3 ft (1 m) and has good disease resistance.

GARDEN USES

'Ballerina' is one of the most useful of all roses. It is perfect for planting in mixed borders alongside a wide range of perennials, bulbs, and shrubs. It works especially well in cottage-style gardens, adding softness and charm. Ideally, place it in a sunny spot at the front or on the corner of a border so it has sufficient space—mature plants are dome-shaped and produce flowers and foliage to ground level. It tolerates some shade during the day and will withstand poor soil. Use it to tumble down a bank, or plant it beside trees as flowering ground cover. It looks good in raised beds, or even spilling out of containers.

CARE AND MAINTENANCE

For best results, give 'Ballerina' a good dose of granular plant food in spring, along with a mulch of well-rotted manure. Deadhead regularly and clear fallen petals from below the plant to reduce disease, particularly if you have less resistant roses nearby. Watch out for aphids and rub them off as soon as they appear. Prune this rose in winter, as for other Group 2 roses, but don't

ALSO TRY

Other shade-tolerant roses include:
• **R. 'Agnes'** is an unusual Rugosa rose with large, pale yellow, well-scented, appealingly unstructured flowers.
• **R. Silas Marner ('Ausraveloe')** has small, soft pink, rosette-form flowers that fade to white at the edges. Good scent.
• **R. 'Hansa'** (pictured above) is vigorous and free-flowering, with well-scented, double, red-purple flowers, followed by red hips.

cut it back too much—trim the branches by no more than a third to an outward-facing bud. It's also a good idea to remove old foliage at this time.

JOIE DE VIVRE

This award-winning rose is perfect for containers—it has a compact habit and repeat-flowers reliably to provide a long season of floral interest. Its lightly scented, peachy pink flowers are sumptuous and large for the size of the plant. They are packed with petals and have an old-fashioned rosette form—perfect if you appreciate the appearance of vintage roses, but are limited for space.

CULTIVAR NAME 'Korfloci 01'
ROSE TYPE Group 2, Patio/Shrub rose
FLOWERING Repeats through summer and into fall
FLOWER SIZE Around 3¼ in (8 cm) across, held in clusters
FLOWER SCENT Light, sweet perfume
VIGOR Average
DISEASE RESISTANCE Excellent
HARDINESS Around −4°F (−20°C)

FEATURES

Raised by acclaimed German rose breeders Kordes in 2010, JOIE DE VIVRE was named Rose of the Year 2011 by the British Association of Rose Breeders. It is a compact plant with healthy, glossy foliage, topped off in summer by old-fashioned blooms, fully double and quartered in form. These are a lustrous peachy pink (the outer petals fading to near-white with age) and have a light, sweet, fruity scent. Deadheading results in more flowers through summer.

Plants reach around 24 in (60 cm) in height and are bushy in habit; the stems are leafy down to ground level. This is a highly disease-resistant rose—another great quality to add to its appeal.

GARDEN USES

If you are looking for a terrific container rose with flowers that have old-fashioned appeal, JOIE DE VIVRE is a perfect pick. Its shrubby, neat habit makes it ideal for a pot, and repeat-flowering means you can enjoy blooms for most of the summer. JOIE DE VIVRE will also thrive in the garden—plant it in a raised bed to bring its flowers closer to eye level or at the front of a mixed border. This is a rose for a sunny spot, although it will tolerate some shade during the day.

JOIE DE VIVRE's peachy-pink flowers have a classic, old-fashioned look.

CARE AND MAINTENANCE

Most people choose JOIE DE VIVRE for a container, but it needs plenty of water to really thrive. Get your plant off to a good start by adding granular fertilizer and top-dressing the container with well-rotted manure each spring, as you would if you planted it in the garden. Every other year, change the top few centimeters of potting mix. Feed your plant throughout the summer months and, once flowering has started, deadhead regularly to produce more flowers. Keep an eye out for aphids (see p.45) and rub them off if they appear. Prune in winter, as for other Group 2 roses.

'RASPBERRY ROYALE'

This attractive plant is one to seek out if you want an easy and reliable rose for a container. 'Raspberry Royale' has good disease resistance and an extended flowering season. From early summer until the first frosts, it bears clusters of lightly perfumed, rounded, bright red, fully double flowers and makes a tidy, bushy shrub. It is also one to consider for growing as a small standard.

CULTIVAR NAME 'Raspberry Royale'
ROSE TYPE Group 2, Patio rose
FLOWERING Repeats through summer and into fall
FLOWER SIZE 1½–2 in (4–5 cm) across, held in showy clusters
FLOWER SCENT Light perfume
VIGOR Average
DISEASE RESISTANCE Good
HARDINESS Around 5°F (−15°C)

Showy, bright red flowers stand out against the glossy, dark green foliage.

FEATURES

Bushy, neat, and disease resistant, this brilliant little rose is also impressively free-flowering and a perfect plant for a pot on a sunny patio. Introduced in 2002 by UK breeder Colin Pearce, it bears showy, quite large sprays of rich red, double, cupped, somewhat ruffled flowers that open from shapely buds held at the tips of upright stems. The blooms will keep on coming as summer passes into fall; the display lasts until the first frosts if the plant is well-fed and deadheaded. 'Raspberry Royale' grows to around 24 in (60 cm) and will tolerate some shade in the day.

GARDEN USES

This is an ideal rose for growing in a container on the terrace or patio as it is neat, compact, and has a long season of interest. It is especially eye-catching when placed in pots on either side of steps, or cascading over a raised urn; elevating the plant brings its lightly fragrant flowers closer for inspection. It is also effective planted as a step-over hedge or massed in a raised bed; it is sometimes sold as a Patio standard.

CARE AND MAINTENANCE

'Raspberry Royale' is generally an easygoing rose—it is disease resistant, so if kept in healthy, active growth, it tends to be problem-free. However, it is important to meet the plant's needs through the growing season. Whether in a pot or planted out, give it plenty of water throughout the summer; in spring, add granular fertilizer and top-dress with well-rotted manure. Keep deadheading the plant for more flowers and watch out for aphids (see p.45), rubbing them off if they appear. Prune as for other Group 2 roses (see p.39).

SWEET MAGIC

This dwarf patio rose is guaranteed to give your garden a hit of vibrant color. Its clustered flowers start out bright orange but fade gracefully to yellow, the petals developing contrasting pinkish tints as they age. With a bushy habit and glossy dark green leaves, this plant will fare well in a container on a sunny patio. Deadhead regularly to encourage the plant to repeat throughout the season.

CULTIVAR NAME 'Dicmagic'
ROSE TYPE Group 2, Patio rose
FLOWERING Repeats through summer and into fall
FLOWER SIZE Around 1½in (4cm) across, held in clusters
FLOWER SCENT Minimal fragrance
VIGOR Average
DISEASE RESISTANCE Good
HARDINESS Around −4°F (−20°C)

Glowing orange blooms slowly fade to a golden yellow with age.

FEATURES

Bred by Dickinson Roses and named Rose of the Year 1987 by the British Association of Rose Breeders, SWEET MAGIC is among the finest of patio roses. Vibrant semi-double, open-cupped blooms begin rich orange and fade to an orange-yellow. The petals take on pinkish tints, giving a two-tone effect when in full flower. This is a bushy plant that reaches a height of 18in (45cm). Deadheading produces flowers into fall. If you stop deadheading toward the end of the season, pretty reddish hips are likely to appear.

GARDEN USES

This is a perfect container rose, sturdy enough to stand variable conditions yet sufficiently compact to fit on a patio and with a long flowering season for great decorative value. Full sun and an open location are essential, but you can group it with other patio roses in separate pots. SWEET MAGIC looks splendid in a sunny corner of a terrace or balcony, or even planted in a raised bed. Plants can be brought inside to grace a cool porch or conservatory while in flower, but move them back outside after flowering and deadhead to allow them to recover.

CARE AND MAINTENANCE

SWEET MAGIC grows well in a pot, but ensure that it has plenty of moisture to avoid the risk of the fungal disease blackspot (see p.44), which causes defoliation and poor flowering. Water daily in hot, dry weather and maintain good hygiene, removing any dropped foliage and debris that may harbor disease. In a bad year, plants may need a spray with fungicide. In spring, feed with granular fertilizer and add a manure top-dressing to the pot. Prune as for other Group 2 roses (see p.39).

ALSO TRY

Other small roses for pots include:
- **R. CAREFREE DAYS ('Meirivoui')** (pictured right) carries beautiful, lightly scented, bright pink flowers that are set against dark leaves.
- **R. QUEEN MOTHER ('Korquemu')** has masses of semi-double light pink flowers held above glossy foliage.
- **R. WILDFIRE ('Fryessex')** has masses of fragrant, bright orange double flowers held in clusters on erect stems above mid-green leaves.

Elegant *Rosa* 'Buff Beauty' is a Hybrid Musk rose that produces heavy trusses of buff- to rose-colored flowers. Many grow it for its delicious scent.

GROUP 3:
OLD GARDEN ROSES

This highly diverse group includes some of the oldest and most distinguished rose cultivars. These exquisite plants may need a little extra care to keep them in top condition, although some are tough and easy to grow. Many are excellent mixers, combining happily with a wide range of garden plants: this helps compensate for the fact that they may flower only once in a year.

'BUFF BEAUTY'

This Hybrid Musk rose is full of classic charm and has been a sought-after selection for decades. It produces trusses of rounded, fully double flowers from plump buds held on elegant arching stems. The blooms are yellowish apricot when they open, and fade slowly to a warm cream hue, releasing a rich Tea rose fragrance all summer. The rose repeat flowers well and tolerates a little shade.

CULTIVAR NAME 'Buff Beauty'
ROSE TYPE Group 3, Hybrid Musk
FLOWERING Repeats through summer and into fall
FLOWER SIZE Around 2¼ in (6 cm) across, held in clusters
FLOWER SCENT Tea rose perfume
VIGOR Strong
DISEASE RESISTANCE Good
HARDINESS Around −4°F (−20°C)

FEATURES

Introduced in 1939 by UK breeder Ann Bentall, this Hybrid Musk rose combines a repeat-flowering habit, excellent fragrance, elegant form, and clusters of soft-hued yellow flowers. The double flowers, while not huge, develop in showy trusses. This rose grows to around 5 ft (1.5 m), with arching stems that can be trained on a wall to make an effective climber. It has good disease resistance and tolerates light shade, making it suitable for mixed plantings.

Glorious yellow-apricot flowers gradually age to a softer yellow.

GARDEN USES

'Buff Beauty' thrives in the sun and is perfect for relaxed planting in cottage-style gardens. It is free-growing, its arching branches becoming weighed down with flowers over the summer. It mixes well with other summer perennials—try oriental poppies, spires of delphiniums and *Eremurus,* or lower geraniums and *Alchemilla.* The globular heads of alliums also look good with this rose. Allow its branches to cascade over low walls or peep through railings, perhaps paired with other Hybrid Musk roses. You can also train it on wires along a sunny wall.

CARE AND MAINTENANCE

'Buff Beauty' is easy is to care for: a dose of granular plant food in spring, along with a mulch of well-rotted manure should keep it healthy. Remove faded individual blooms in early summer and deadhead swiftly after the first flowers to prompt more blooms later. Clear away dropped petals after the flowers fade. Some blackspot (see p.44) is likely to occur, especially in dry summers, but is easily controlled. Watch for aphids on new growth and rub off. With its elegant habit, this rose is best with little or no pruning, apart from the removal of damaged or diseased wood, but if space is an issue, simply prune to shape.

'CHARLES DE MILLS'

This sumptuous antique rose produces beautifully formed, rosette-shaped flowers in early summer. The masses of tightly packed, reddish magenta-pink petals provide a wondrous old rose perfume. It makes a vigorous, leafy, upright, then arching shrub, and has reasonable disease resistance, growing well even in a little shade and mixing well with other plants.

CULTIVAR NAME 'Charles de Mills'
ROSE TYPE Group 3, Gallica
FLOWERING Just once, in early summer
FLOWER SIZE Around 3¼–4 in (8–10 cm) across, singly or in small clusters
FLOWER SCENT Good, old rose perfume
VIGOR Average
DISEASE RESISTANCE Fair
HARDINESS Around −4°F (−20°C)

Densely packed flower heads are held on thornless stems.

FEATURES

Grown in gardens since the late 18th century, possibly earlier, this superb selection is one of the finest Gallica roses. The large magenta-pink double flowers are beautifully quartered, and have densely packed petals. The blooms are often perfectly circular and appear flattened. When fully open, a little green eye peeks from the center of the bloom, which has a rich old rose scent. The plant is typically leafy, with dark green foliage and vigorous growth. The thornless stems are upright to around 5 ft (1.5 m). Plants may develop an arching habit with age, and sucker from the base.

GARDEN USES

This plant fares well in full sun or part shade in well-drained, fertile soils and tolerates a little competition, making it great for mixing with other plants at the back of borders. Its character suits the relaxed style of cottage gardens. Flowering through June and July means it can be used with summer favorites, such as purple foxgloves and *Campanula*, or with a froth of green *Alchemilla* at the base. It also grows well with other shrubs, including arching *Philadelphus* or *Deutzia*. You can even use it as an informal flowering hedge. The flowers look pretty in a small vase.

CARE AND MAINTENANCE

This rose grows happily in a range of situations and is very popular even though its flowering season is more limited than that of many modern roses. Apply granular plant food in spring and mulch with rotted manure—it likes fertile soil. Rub off aphids if they appear. In a wet year, mildew can affect plants (see p.44), so you may need to spray with fungicide. Prune in summer after flowering; deadhead, and tidy around the plant. Blackspot can occur in dry summers. Cut out any dead, damaged, rubbing, or diseased wood, and thin stems if overcrowded. Don't overdo it: these roses need little pruning.

ALSO TRY

Other beautifully scented Group 3 roses include:.
- *R.* 'Roseraie de l'Hay' is an easy Rugosa rose with loose, rich magenta double flowers that have a sensationally powerful scent. It repeats well.
- *R.* 'Königin von Dänemark' (pictured below) has beautiful, soft pink flowers with a richer hue at the heart of the bloom. Its old rose perfume is swoon-worthy.
- *R.* 'Madame Boll' (syn. 'Comte de Chambord') is a Damask Portland rose with pink, highly scented flowers.

'CORNELIA'

This easy-to-grow **Hybrid Musk** rose bears trusses of gorgeous double peach-pink flowers from early summer. Its displays are often at their most impressive in the fall, when the fragrant blooms—held against bronze-tinted foliage on elegant, arching stems—appear in glorious profusion and inject color and scent into the garden just as other plants are starting to die back.

CULTIVAR NAME 'Cornelia'
ROSE TYPE Group 3, Hybrid Musk
FLOWERING Repeats through summer and into fall
FLOWER SIZE 2 in (5 cm) across, held in clusters
FLOWER SCENT Tea rose perfume
VIGOR Strong
DISEASE RESISTANCE Good
HARDINESS Around −4°F (−20°C)

The small peachy-pink flowers often attract pollinating insects.

FEATURES

Introduced by the "father of Hybrid Musk roses," Joseph Pemberton, in 1925, 'Cornelia' ranks as one of his finest selections and is still popular. Its unusual flowers—individually small yet double and open-faced—are held in large tresses. They emerge from plump, rounded buds and are warm peach-pink, the tone becoming pinker with age. The summer display is attractive, but the cooler, wetter conditions of fall seem to rejuvenate the plant: its musk-scented flowers glow amid the profusion of the season and appear until the first frosts. Plants are large, reaching around 6 ft (1.8 m), the foliage distinctly bronze-green and the growth attractively arching.

GARDEN USES

This is an easy plant, reveling in sun but also thriving in some shade. It is large and needs space, so plant it toward the back of a border. At its best in the fall, pair it with similarly late performers, such as asters and other seasonal daisies, Japanese anemones, and ornamental grasses. It can also hold its own with striking plants such as cannas, *Eucomis*, and gingers, which peak at this time. Equally, it looks at home in a traditional cottage-garden setting. You can plant it as a flowering hedge or train the stems on a wall as a small climber.

CARE AND MAINTENANCE

Give 'Cornelia' granular plant food and a mulch of manure in spring. This is an easy rose, but it needs some care. Watch for aphids in spring and rub them off if they appear. When in flower, remove faded blooms; after the first flush fades, deadhead swiftly for good reflowering. Clear around the plants to reduce the risk of disease: blackspot may occur, especially in dry summers, but is easily controlled on this rose (see p.44). With its naturally arching habit, this plant needs little or no pruning.

ALSO TRY

Other great Hybrid Musk roses are:
- **R. 'Penelope'** is a vigorous plant with great perfume that bears masses of pink-tinged white flowers held in impressive heads. These are followed by coral-colored hips that are a valuable food source for birds.
- **R. 'Prosperity'** (pictured right) has double, creamy white fragrant flowers held in large clusters at the ends of elegant, arching stems.

'FANTIN-LATOUR'

The shapely rosette-formed flowers of this ravishing plant are typical of old-fashioned roses. They are at their most glorious in full bloom during early summer, when they appear in a delicate shade of soft blush pink. These petal-packed flowers also come with a knockout perfume—among the most famed of all roses—making this plant worth a little effort to grow well.

CULTIVAR NAME 'Fantin-Latour'
ROSE TYPE Group 3, Centifolia
FLOWERING Just once a year, in early summer
FLOWER SIZE Around 4 in (10 cm) across, held in clusters
FLOWER SCENT Superb, powerful, sweet perfume
VIGOR Average
DISEASE RESISTANCE Tolerable
HARDINESS Around −4°F (−20°C)

FEATURES

This plant is one of the Centifolia or Provence roses, many of which are thought to date from at least the 17th century. 'Fantin-Latour' itself has been highly regarded since the first half of the 20th century. The plant's large, cupped, pastel-pink double flowers are exquisitely scented and appear from reddish buds; the color is richest in the center of the bloom. The plant is large, growing to around 5 ft (1.5 m), and may need support—in full and generous flower, the thorny, somewhat arching branches are often weighed down.

GARDEN USES

In early summer, this sensational rose makes a wonderful contribution to the garden. It should do well in some shade, as long as the soil is fertile and well-drained and the site reasonably open. The plant is vigorous enough to grow toward the back of a mixed border, but make sure that the competition is not too fierce. The delicate pink flowers pair well with silver-leaved plants, such as *Artemisia* and *Senecio*, and blend perfectly with blue flowers, including *Nepeta*, *Baptisia*, and lavender; it also looks great with pink or white peonies. Against a wall, the stems can be trained like those of a climber. Cut flowers look especially attractive in a small vase.

Blush pink blooms are magnificently offset by the plant's lush, apple-green foliage.

CARE AND MAINTENANCE

'Fantin-Latour' needs attention but is little trouble once happily established. It likes fertile soil, so apply granular feed and plenty of well-rotted manure in spring. Rub off any aphids. In a wet year, watch for mildew (*see p.44*); you may need to spray. If rain persists, some flowers may not open. Remove faded blooms and clear dropped petals. Blackspot may occur in dry summers. Plants may also need support. Prune directly after flowering—take out dead, damaged, rubbing, or diseased wood, and thin the stems only if overcrowded.

'FELICIA'

This elegant rose has become deservedly popular. It bears impressive heads of strongly scented, soft pink double flowers in early summer, repeating the show in the fall. Like many other Hybrid Musk roses it is vigorous, shrugs off disease well, and is easy to grow in sun or light shade; what's more, it is great for mixing with other shrubs or perennials in garden borders.

CULTIVAR NAME 'Felicia'
ROSE TYPE Group 3, Hybrid Musk
FLOWERING Early summer and again in the fall
FLOWER SIZE 2–2¼in (5–6cm) across, held in clusters
FLOWER SCENT Tea rose perfume
VIGOR Strong
DISEASE RESISTANCE Good
HARDINESS Around −4°F (−20°C)

The flowers are wonderfully varied in tint and nod from upright stems.

GARDEN USES

Large-growing 'Felicia' favors full sun but will stand light shade, so it is a good choice for the back of a border. It mixes well with summer-flowering perennials and is great as part of a pastel color scheme in a cottage garden. To achieve this look, combine it with beautiful spires of delphiniums, lupins, and foxgloves. You can also use it in island beds, where it can be easily underplanted with low-growing perennials such as *Nepeta* or geraniums. This rose is also perfect for injecting a burst of color into shrub plantings. Alternatively, train it on a wall as a climber or grow it as a flowering hedge.

CARE AND MAINTENANCE

Give 'Felicia' granular plant food in spring along with a mulch of well-rotted manure or garden compost. Rub off any aphids and, during flowering, remove faded blooms to keep the flower heads fresh. Deadhead swiftly after the first flush to produce more blooms. Clear away any dropped petals to reduce disease. Some blackspot can occur if the summer is dry, but it is easily controlled on this plant (see *p.44*). Its elegant habit means that this rose is best with little or no pruning, other than the removal of damaged or diseased wood.

FEATURES

Introduced in 1928 by British breeder Joseph Pemberton, 'Felicia' has gorgeous double flowers held in clusters, which it produces freely through the season. The blooms open in a soft pink color and the outer petals gradually fade closer to white with age; they have a musky Tea rose scent. The plant is well-shaped, bushy, and vigorous, reaching heights of around 5ft (1.5m). It has long arching stems that are well covered with rich green foliage.

'FERDINAND PICHARD'

The pink flowers of this luxurious Bourbon rose are boldly striped with shades of crimson and purple, making it a splendid and unusual sight in summer. It will repeat flower reliably later in the season if deadheaded. Use this compact, thorny plant to bring variety to rose gardens and inject interest into mixed borders; it gives great value and proves healthy and quite easy to grow.

CULTIVAR NAME 'Ferdinand Pichard'
ROSE TYPE Group 3, Bourbon
FLOWERING Early summer and again in fall
FLOWER SIZE Around 2¾–3¼ in (7–8 cm) across, held in clusters
FLOWER SCENT Delicious fruity perfume
VIGOR Average
DISEASE RESISTANCE Good
HARDINESS Around −4°F (−20°C)

FEATURES

Raised in France and introduced in 1910 by Rémi Tanne, 'Ferdinand Pichard' is an exciting and distinctive garden rose. The double flowers are glorious: quite cupped and rounded at first, they become more open-centered with age. The pinkish-white petals are striped, dashed, and dotted with raspberry-red and magenta and have a great fruity perfume. Lush, apple-green foliage provides the perfect backdrop for these striking flowers, which are not too prone to rain damage. Deadheading produces more blooms at the end of the summer. It is a bushy plant with thorny stems and grows to around 4 ft (1.2 m).

This rose's flamboyant blooms have a wonderful fruity perfume.

GARDEN USES

'Ferdinand Pichard' is not too fussy about soil, but likes a warm, sunny, sheltered spot in the garden. Choose this striking rose to add drama toward the front of existing rose borders or as a talking point within a mixed planting: plant it where the flowers can be easily admired for their patterns and scent, and where it will not be overshadowed in terms of light and beauty. Some gardeners train it as a small climber on a wall or grow it with the support of an obelisk. It also makes a great flowering hedge.

CARE AND MAINTENANCE

This is an easy, strong-growing rose. Give it a good dose of granular plant food in spring, along with a mulch of well-rotted manure or garden compost. Rub off any aphids that may appear. Remove faded blooms and clear away any dropped petals to reduce the risk of disease and promote reflowering. Although the plant has good disease resistance, blackspot can occur in dry summers (see p.44); pick off the worst-affected leaves and resort to fungicide spray only if necessary. This rose needs minimal pruning, other than the removal of old, damaged, or diseased wood; reduce stems by about one third in late winter.

ALSO TRY

Other striped roses in Group 3 are:
- **R. 'Camayeux'** is a Gallica rose. It has fully double, pale pink blooms with purple stripes that are held on arching stems.
- **R. 'Honorine de Brabant'** is a large, bushy Bourbon rose with rounded, rather cupped, pale pink double flowers striped with magenta. It repeats well.
- **R. 'Variegata di Bologna'** (pictured above) is an exquisite Bourbon rose. It has large, cupped, blush-pink double flowers that are randomly striped with purple-red.

RED ROSE OF LANCASTER

This rose was the symbol of the House of Lancaster in its struggle for the English throne in the 15th century. It is also known as the apothecary's rose for its medicinal qualities—it reportedly has anti-inflammatory and antibacterial properties. In the garden, it is an impressively tough and disease-resistant plant that is easy to grow, producing multitudes of vibrant red-pink semi-double flowers.

SPECIES NAME *Rosa gallica* var. *officinalis*

ROSE TYPE Group 3, Gallica

FLOWERING Just once a year, in early summer

FLOWER SIZE Around 3¼ in (8 cm) across, held in clusters

FLOWER SCENT Old rose perfume

VIGOR Strong growing

DISEASE RESISTANCE Good

HARDINESS −4°F (−20°C) or lower

FEATURES

The origins of this historic rose are lost to the mists of time but it was probably brought to Gaul (France) from the east by the Romans. Leafy and compact, it grows to around 4 ft (1.2 m) and is covered in large, bright red-pink, semi-double, open-centered flowers with golden stamens. Its blooms attract pollinators and have some scent; they may be followed by reddish hips. This rose has a tendency to form suckers (shoots from the rootstock, see p.22).

This long-cultivated rose makes a dramatic entrance in early summer.

GARDEN USES

This is a tough plant that stands poor soils and cold conditions. Despite its ancient origins, it is suited to modern gardens. It is a great mixer and useful in borders and beds with a range of other plants. Let it mingle with early summer-flowering perennials such as geraniums, campanulas, lupins, and *Astrantia*—it looks impressive at the front of a border as it is well clothed with foliage low down. Try it in relatively shaded spots, as long as the site is fairly open and gets an hour or two of sun a day. Use it as a structural centerpiece in an herb garden or in pollinator-friendly plantings. It is great in a flowering hedge and will even thrive in a large pot.

CARE AND MAINTENANCE

Red Rose of Lancaster is one of the easiest of roses. Provide granular plant food in spring, along with a mulch of well-rotted manure or garden compost; rub off any aphids that appear around this time. You won't need to deadhead and you can expect reddish hips later on. Tidy up the plant in summer: after flowering, take out dead, damaged, rubbing, or diseased wood, and thin the stems, if overcrowded. Do not prune unless the plant is too big. This rose is disease resistant, but take off any black-spotted leaves that may appear.

ROSA MUNDI

This famous antique selection is said to be named after "fair Rosamund," the mistress of 12th-century English king, Henry II. It has been much admired by gardeners for centuries for its dramatically striped, semi-double, fragrant pink-and-white flowers. Despite its delicate demeanor, it is a hardy, disease-resistant, easy-to-grow rose that is a great addition to early summer gardens.

CULTIVAR NAME *Rosa gallica* var. *versicolor*
ROSE TYPE Group 3, Gallica
FLOWERING? Just once a year, in early summer
FLOWER SIZE Around 3¼ in (8 cm) across, held in clusters
FLOWER SCENT Old rose perfume
VIGOR Strong growing
DISEASE RESISTANCE Good
HARDINESS −4°F (−20°C) or lower

A vibrant classic that is tough, lightly scented, and a magnet for pollinators.

FEATURES

This spectacular rose appeared as a variant of *Rosa gallica* var. *officinalis* (*see left*) around 500 years ago, when its patterned flowers would have been unique in gardens. Opening in early summer, each delicate white petal is striped, spotted, and dashed with red-pink. The flowers have some scent and may be followed in the fall by hips. This is an easy, occasionally suckering shrub that reaches around 4 ft (1.2 m), growing well in sun or light shade; it withstands cold and poor soil, and is seldom affected by disease.

GARDEN USES

In early summer, this rose makes a truly spectacular centerpiece to a cottage-garden style mixed border. Its vibrant flowers work particularly well among blush- or silvery pinks. If possible, position this leafy rose toward the front of a planting so its striking blooms can be properly admired.

Rosa Mundi will grow well in relatively shady spots, as long as the site is open and receives an hour or two of sun a day. In these situations, it looks superb backed by contemporary foliage-rich plantings of ferns and Solomon's seal. This is also a great rose for growing with herbs and as a flowering hedge; it will thrive in a large container, too.

CARE AND MAINTENANCE

In spring, provide *Rosa* Mundi with granular plant food and a mulch of well-rotted manure or garden compost. Rub off any aphids, which often attack in spring. Avoid deadheading if you want to enjoy the orange hips in the fall. Tidy the plant after flowering by taking out dead, damaged, rubbing, or diseased wood, and thin the stems if they become overcrowded. Do not prune unless the plant is getting too big for your liking. This sturdy rose has good disease resistance, but remove any black-spotted leaves that may develop. If non-striped flowers appear, remove the growth they were produced on—this rose can revert.

ALSO TRY

Other Gallica roses include:
- **R. 'Complicata'** (pictured right) has masses of large, single, bright pink flowers with a pale heart. It is vigorous-growing and may produce displays of hips in the fall.
- **R. 'Ipsilante'** has lustrous, soft pink double flowers, with great perfume, held on arching stems.
- **R. 'Tuscany Superb'** displays dark red semi-double flowers, each with a central mass of golden stamens.

RED-LEAVED ROSE

This unusual species rose is grown for its overall appeal rather than just its blooms. The delicate foliage, held on arching stems, has a striking, shimmering, silver-purple hue. In summer, the plant is studded with small, single, mauve-pink flowers, which are followed in the fall by displays of red hips. It is a tough customer, standing a range of conditions including some shade and dry soil.

SPECIES NAME *Rosa glauca*
ROSE TYPE Group 3, Species rose
FLOWERING Just once a year, in early summer
FLOWER SIZE Around 1½in (4cm) across in small clusters
FLOWER SCENT Minimal fragrance
VIGOR Strong
DISEASE RESISTANCE Good
HARDINESS −4°F (−20°C) or lower

The plant's vibrant, rose-pink flowers are a magnet for pollinators.

FEATURES

Native to Europe and introduced to cultivation in 1830, this useful and distinctive rose species has become popular in recent years. Gardeners appreciate its long period of interest: initially, with its red-backed metallic foliage in spring and early summer; then, displays of single, yellow-centered pink flowers; and finally, clusters of orange-red hips that last through the fall. The long, upright, then arching stems reach around 6½ft (2m) tall. The starlike flowers open from early summer to midsummer. The plant is robust, being highly tolerant of poor soil, light shade, and dry conditions.

GARDEN USES

This rose is a great choice for an area where silvery leaves are required—perhaps to combine with a pastel-themed planting or to bring depth to a predominantly white garden. Its tolerance of dry, poor soils also makes it ideal in graveled areas, especially where trees cast problematic shade on these typically sun-drenched spots. The plant's arching growth makes it best-suited to informal areas. Its spherical hips can also help boost fall interest alongside drifts of asters or Japanese anemones.

CARE AND MAINTENANCE

This rose needs remarkably little attention. In spring, give it a feed with granular fertilizer and mulch around the roots. It has good disease resistance and does not need deadheading. The plant does not require regular pruning either—indeed reducing its stems will only spoil its graceful form. On mature plants, however, you should cut down old stems to the base of the plant in late winter to generate new growth from the ground.

'MADAME HARDY'

An old rose to treasure, this superb Damask produces perfectly shaped, rosette-form, glowing white flowers in great quantities. The large blooms are deliciously scented and have a distinctive green "eye." Although antique, the plant is surprisingly disease resistant, reliable, and easy to keep; it can even be trained along wires on a fence or wall as a small climber.

CULTIVAR NAME 'Madame Hardy'
ROSE TYPE Group 3, Damask
FLOWERING Just once a year, in early summer
FLOWER SIZE Around 4 in (10 cm) across, held in clusters
FLOWER SCENT Powerful old rose scent
VIGOR Strong growing
DISEASE RESISTANCE Good
HARDINESS –4°F (–20°C) or lower

FEATURES

'Madame Hardy' was raised by French grower Julien-Alexandre Hardy, and introduced in 1832. The blooms have superb fragrance and are large, fully double, and cupped at first with a rosette form. A hint of pink warms the petals initially, but with age they open flat and turn pure white, displaying a little green eye at the center. The plant has slightly thorny, erect stems to 5 ft (1.5 m) tall, and lush, bright green foliage.

White blooms, tinged with pink at this stage, contrast with bright green foliage.

GARDEN USES

'Madame Hardy' is not a fussy rose and stands poor soil and a range of sites. With its somewhat open form, this rose suits country and cottage gardens and, tolerating some shade, also grows well with other plants in borders. It looks great amid pastel hues and is perfect for an all-white border, or planting that will be admired in the evening, when the spectacular white blooms seem to glow. Its form depends on how you prune it—once established, it can be kept neater and will then fit into more formal situations. If you plant this rose against a wall or fence it can be pruned and trained as a climber, reaching around 6½ ft (2 m). The clusters of flowers look charming in a small vase.

CARE AND MAINTENANCE

For best results, apply granular plant food in spring, then mulch with well-rotted manure or garden compost. Rub off aphids from flower buds if they appear. During flowering, remove faded blooms to keep the plant fresh; after flowering, clear around the plant; then prune lightly, removing weak, rubbing, diseased, or dead stems. If the plant gets too big for your liking, cut stems back by a third. Some disease may occur in dry summers, but can be controlled by removing the affected growth.

ALSO TRY

Other white- or cream-flowering Group 3 roses include:
- *R. alba* **'Alba Maxima'** is a large-growing shrub that has masses of scented, quite loose but charming double white flowers.
- *R. centifolia* **'Shailer's White Moss'** has an old rose fragrance. Its pale pink double flowers open from mossy buds and turn white as they mature.
- *R.* **'Boule de Neige'** (pictured above) is a charming Bourbon rose with clusters of rounded, small, white double blooms that have great scent.

Elegant *Rosa* 'Felicia' bears clusters of scented flowers through summer and into fall. It repeats well and holds its own in mixed plantings.

'MUTABILIS'

This distinctive plant makes a great addition to almost any garden because it is among the longest-flowering of roses. Its slender stems support glossy, red-tinged foliage and airy heads of delicate single flowers composed of five dainty, fluttering petals. Blooms open apricot-orange but age to a warm red-pink, providing multicolored displays almost year-round.

CULTIVAR NAME *Rosa* x *odorata* 'Mutabilis'
ROSE TYPE Group 3, China rose
FLOWERING Repeats from mid-spring into winter
FLOWER SIZE Around 2¾ in (7 cm) across, usually in small clusters
FLOWER SCENT Minimal fragrance
VIGOR Strong growing
DISEASE RESISTANCE Excellent
HARDINESS Around 14°F (–10°C)

FEATURES

This rose produces clusters of flowers with crumpled, then fluttery petals for much of the year. They open yellow-orange, and become richer in hue before developing pinkish tints, and turning red-pink before petals fall. The first flush in spring is profuse but the rose will continue flowering into a mild winter. The plant is shrubby, reaching 3 ft (1 m) or more if grown up a wall.

GARDEN USES

This is a useful and versatile rose that mixes well with other plants. Grow it in a warm, sunny spot where it is sheltered from the elements—beside a wall, where it can be trained as a climber, is best. Use it to add color to Mediterranean plantings—its flowers look perfect with *Cistus*. Alternatively, plant it within mixed borders—its continual flowering makes it a good candidate to anchor a design. 'Mutabilis' is a free-growing plant so it is not suited to formal areas, however it looks superb cascading over a low wall or on a terrace.

CARE AND MAINTENANCE

This is an easy rose to grow and not much troubled by pests and diseases. Winter hardiness can be an issue, so planting it in a sheltered spot is key. Feed in spring with granular fertilizer and mulch well. Deadheading is certainly worth the effort to promote more flowers, but pruning can be kept to a minimum. After a while, the plant may get large and twiggy—if this happens, cut it back quite hard in late winter, although the earliest flowers may be delayed by this treatment.

'Mutabilis' is a marvelous rose of great antiquity, long grown in Chinese gardens.

'BENGAL CRIMSON'

This rose provides almost constant color in the garden. It produces its blood-red flowers throughout the year in the mildest gardens, and elsewhere flowering pauses only for three of the coldest months. Its single blooms open from pointed buds and often appear in astonishing profusion. The plant is highly disease-resistant, easy to grow, and may be free-standing or trained on a wall.

CULTIVAR NAME *Rosa* x *odorata* (Sanguinea Group) 'Bengal Crimson'
ROSE TYPE Group 3, China rose
FLOWERING Repeats from mid-spring into winter
FLOWER SIZE Around 3¼ in (8 cm) across, usually in small clusters
FLOWER SCENT No fragrance
VIGOR Strong growing
DISEASE RESISTANCE Excellent
HARDINESS Around 14°F (−10°C)

FEATURES

'Bengal Crimson' has a nearly unrivaled flowering season and its almost thorn-free stems may be virtually evergreen. From mid-spring until after Christmas it will—in milder areas—produce a succession of single, five-petaled flowers: blood-red and uneven in size, these surround a gold crown and open from pointed buds held in clusters. Flowering is usually arrested over winter. It can easily reach 6½ ft (2 m) as a free-standing shrub. It is simple to grow this rose from cuttings.

GARDEN USES

This easy plant is ideal for adding cross-seasonal color to beds and borders. In spring, it looks great paired with lime-green *Euphorbia characias,* and in summer with sultry *Cotinus* 'Royal Purple'. At summer's end, it pairs well with fiery dahlias, salvias, and kniphofia; and it will hold its own through fall alongside asters, Japanese anemones, euonymus, and acers.

This antique selection is not very hardy, so plant it by a wall in cooler areas or keep it under glass in a conservatory or greenhouse as long as summer conditions are not too hot. Training on a free-standing trellis, a wall, or a fence will help impose order on this plant's free-growing habit.

Characterful crimson blooms contrast well with gray-green foliage.

CARE AND MAINTENANCE

If you garden in a mild area, this rose could not be simpler to keep. It has no disease problems and aphids seldom bother it. Feed in spring with granular fertilizer and mulch it well. Deadheading regularly promotes more flowers. Pruning should be minimal, though you may sometimes need to give mature plants a harder prune to keep them in bounds. Do this in late winter; you will lose early flowers, but the plant will soon recover.

WINGED THORN ROSE

This rose is an unusual but interesting choice, chiefly because its thorns—usually the bane of gardeners—are its main attraction, especially in the winter when they provide a splash of color. Winged, translucent, and ruby-red, the thorns stud the plant's upright stems and sit alongside delicate, fernlike foliage and pretty, white, summer flowers, which release a delicate fragrance.

CULTIVAR NAME *Rosa sericea* subsp. *omeiensis* f. *pteracantha* 'Lutea'
ROSE TYPE Group 3, Species rose
FLOWERING Just once a year, in summer
FLOWER SIZE Around 1½ in (4 cm) across
FLOWER SCENT Delicate fragrance
VIGOR Strong growing
DISEASE RESISTANCE Excellent
HARDINESS Around −4°F (−20°C)

The plant's simple, gold-stamened white flowers attract many pollinators.

Impressive thorns, with huge bases, are the main feature of this plant.

FEATURES

This rose reaches heights of around 8 ft (2.5 m). Its stems are initially erect, but arch with age, eventually forming a suckering thicket. The stems are armed with bristles as well as the extraordinary thorns. On young growth, the thorns are ruby-red and translucent but they later develop the color of parchment. The leaves are delicate and fernlike. In early summer, four-petaled white flowers with gold stamens open. These are flat at first but become cupped with age. They are followed by globular orange hips.

GARDEN USES

Plant this rose where its stems will be backlit by morning or evening sun. An open, sunny site with little competition from other plants is ideal. You can plant grasses and shorter perennials around the base, or position the rose at the back of a border, as long as it is open to the sun. By winter, the red color has largely faded, but the huge thorns are still of interest when beside *Cornus*, *Rubus*, or other red-stemmed plants.

CARE AND MAINTENANCE

This plant is grown in a different way to other roses. The objective is to produce as many young stems as possible and thereby optimize the displays of thorns. When established, you can treat it as a coppice and cut everything down in late winter—but older growth bears flowers, so if you enjoy these, you must achieve a balance. Either cut out a proportion (around a third) in late winter, or prune the whole plant hard after flowering. Feed in spring with granular fertilizer, and mulch well to help promote good growth. This plant seldom suffers from disease.

'PERLE D'OR'

This long-flowering rose deserves to be planted more often because of its interesting character. It has small apricot and pink flowers that appear in showy clusters; as they age, their outer petals fold back, creating a pompom shape. The plant is disease resistant, easy to grow, and thrives in a warm, sunny site. It is suitable for planting in borders or against walls, and will adapt to life in a large pot.

CULTIVAR NAME 'Perle d'Or'
ROSE TYPE Group 3, China/Polyantha
FLOWERING Repeats through summer and into fall
FLOWER SIZE Around 2 in (5 cm) across, held in clusters
FLOWER SCENT Light, sweet perfume
VIGOR Strong growing
DISEASE RESISTANCE Good
HARDINESS Around 5°F (−15°C)

FEATURES

This plant is a hybrid between a Tea and Polyantha rose but is often classed among the latter (Group 2). However, its size and habit fit better with Group 3 roses. It was bred by French grower Joseph Rambaux and introduced in 1883. The small, lightly scented flowers appear in bunches and initially resemble miniature Hybrid Tea blooms, with their pointed, high centers. They become more rosette shaped with age, changing color from warm peach to pink, then cream in the process. The plant is healthy, bushy, and vigorous, almost thorn-free, with dark foliage. It reaches 6 ft (1.8 m) or more against a wall.

GARDEN USES

This rose should be more popular because it has a long flowering period, teamed with great vigor and disease resistance. It does, however, need a lot of sun and a sheltered position, so is ideal for a border backed by a wall. The flower color means it fits well in warm-themed plantings alongside other yellow and orange blooms. However, it can also be used to warm up cooler pastel schemes. It is glorious beside lime-green *Euphorbia* x *pasteurii*. You can grow this rose in a large container; its generous flowering means it looks stunning on a terrace or patio.

CARE AND MAINTENANCE

'Perle d'Or' will flower for months if deadheaded. Give it granular plant food in spring, followed by a mulch of well-rotted manure or garden compost. As the year progresses, rub off any aphids and remove faded blooms; deadhead after flowering for more blooms. Feed and water regularly if in a pot. It needs little pruning, apart from the removal of damaged or diseased wood; shape the plants lightly when deadheading to keep within bounds. Disease is unusual.

This fine rose can be grown in a border, on a wall, or in a large pot.

WHITE JAPANESE ROSE

This virtually indestructible rose thrives in poor soil and needs remarkably little care. It offers well-scented, pure white flowers throughout summer and then goes on to impress even further with masses of showy hips during fall. It makes a great hedge plant, flourishes in coastal areas that defeat other roses, and is great for a wildlife garden, attracting a diversity of pollinators.

CULTIVAR NAME *Rosa rugosa* 'Alba'
ROSE TYPE Group 3, Rugosa
FLOWERING Repeats through summer and into fall
FLOWER SIZE Around 3½in (9cm) across, held in small clusters
FLOWER SCENT Strong old rose perfume
VIGOR Strong
DISEASE RESISTANCE Excellent
HARDINESS Around −4°F (−20°C)

With its cast-iron constitution, this plant shrugs off mistreatment and disease.

FEATURES

There are few roses that can compete with this plant for the glory of its shining hips, but it has many other great features, too. It grows in the poorest soil, reaching around 4ft (1.2m), suckering merrily, even in sand dunes. The spiny, bushy plant flowers all summer, its blooms opening from pinkish buds. These are followed by its signature scarlet hips, often alongside the scented white flowers. Both are displayed beautifully against soft green foliage that turns butter yellow in fall.

GARDEN USES

This is a rose that can survive uncared-for in parking lots and municipal plantings: it will grow almost anywhere, except waterlogged soil or deep shade. Its somewhat rustic appearance and suckering habit means it suits wilder locations well, but it can also look great in gravel gardens, cottage gardens, or repeated as clumps in more formal borders, especially where fall color from flowers, hips, and finally foliage is needed. This rose also makes a superbly thorny flowering hedge, even for the most exposed locations.

CARE AND MAINTENANCE

Once established, this rose can survive with little care, but it will become much more impressive if given a little more attention. Provide it with granular plant food in spring along with a mulch of well-rotted manure, then stand back and leave it to perform—don't attempt to deadhead.

Plants only need pruning to keep them in shape, although you may sometimes need to remove dead wood from the thicket of stems. If the plants grow too large after a few years, you can renovate them by pruning all stems to around 6in (15cm) from the ground in late winter. Disease is rarely an issue with this rose.

ALSO TRY

Roses with impressive hips include:
- *R. moyesii* 'Geranium' (pictured below) has red single flowers, followed by crops of gorgeous, elongated, orange-red hips. It forms a large, spreading plant.
- *R.* Tottering-by-Gently ('Auscartoon') is a charming David Austin introduction with masses of yellow single flowers in summer, followed by orange hips.
- *R.* 'Fru Dagmar Hastrup' is a Rugosa rose with pink single flowers produced over a long season, followed by large dark red hips, often alongside the blooms.

'TUSCANY SUPERB'

This Gallica rose has a truly regal appearance. It produces irresistible dark red semi-double flowers that have a contrasting central boss of golden stamens. The blooms, lightly scented and offset by dark foliage, are held on upright, almost thorn-free stems. It has proved to be a good choice for mixed borders, standing light shade and doing well alongside other plants.

CULTIVAR NAME 'Tuscany Superb'
ROSE TYPE Group 3, Gallica
FLOWERING Just once a year, in early summer
FLOWER SIZE Around 3½ in (9 cm) across, singly or in clusters
FLOWER SCENT Old rose perfume
VIGOR Average
DISEASE RESISTANCE Good
HARDINESS −4°F (−20°C) or lower

Voluptuous, velvety blooms are displayed against a bed of lush foliage.

FEATURES

'Tuscany Superb' was bred by UK rose grower Thomas Rivers and introduced in 1837. If you are keen on rich, saturated colors, this is the rose for you. Blooms appear in early summer, often in small groups: they are large, semi-double, and have ruffled petals of dark magenta-red. At the heart of each flower are yellow stamens, which stand out like a golden crown against a velvet robe. If you avoid deadheading, the flowers are followed by decorative hips. The plant is quite compact and rounded, yet upright to around 4 ft (1.2 m), and is virtually thorn-free.

GARDEN USES

With its superb flowers, this rose grows well in mixed borders, adding a rich depth to paler plantings: it works perfectly alongside silvery foliage and pastel hues. Shade-tolerance makes it a particularly useful plant for adding to existing plantings, either in the middle or toward the front of a border. It also suits relaxed plantings of old roses, perhaps in wilder parts of the garden, or within an existing herb garden; it is a suitable candidate for an informal flowering hedge.

CARE AND MAINTENANCE

'Tuscany Superb' finds a home in many modern gardens, even though it does not repeat flower. It is a straightforward plant, but needs a little attention. Give it granular food in spring and mulch well with rotted manure or garden compost. Prune right after flowering; tidy around the plant but avoid total deadheading as you will sacrifice the hips. Rub off any aphids. Mildew may strike in a wet year (see p.44); cut out dead, damaged, rubbing, or diseased wood, and thin stems if overcrowded.

ALSO TRY

Try these other great Gallica hybrids:
- **R. 'Cardinal de Richelieu'** (pictured right) has impressive double rosette flowers of rich purple with a sweet scent on a compact, bushy plant.
- **R. 'Belle de Crécy'** is a large arching plant with pink-purple, fully double rosette-form flowers.
- **R. 'James Mason'** is a semi-double selection with bright red flowers and great fall hips.

'WILLIAM LOBB'

Vigorous and generous in bloom, this antique rose bears large sprays of superbly fragrant, semi-double flowers. These open from appealing fuzzy buds that look as though they are covered in moss and give the plants great character. It is a tall-growing rose, the arching stems of which benefit from support. It works well trained on a wall as a climber or used within mixed borders.

CULTIVAR NAME 'William Lobb'
ROSE TYPE Group 3, Moss rose
FLOWERING Just once a year, in early summer
FLOWER SIZE Around 4 in (10 cm) across, held in clusters
FLOWER SCENT Powerful old-rose scent
VIGOR Strong
DISEASE RESISTANCE Fair
HARDINESS −4°F (−20°C) or lower

FEATURES

Moss roses, which have buds covered in aromatic, mosslike growth, were popular in the 19th century. Many selections, including 'William Lobb', were bred in France. This plant, introduced in 1855, is one of the best-known and easiest of the type. It is a vigorous-growing rose with tall, prickly stems that often reach 6½ ft (2 m) tall. The semi-double rosette-shaped blooms are plentiful in early summer. Purple-pink in hue, sometimes with a gray-violet tinge, they are held in large clusters that have a powerful old-rose fragrance.

GARDEN USES

With its tall-growing habit, 'William Lobb' should be carefully placed in the garden—correctly positioned, it is impressive, but it can look untidy. It tolerates shade and needs support—in relaxed, informal gardens, this could come from other roses or shrubs; its branches can then be allowed to arch down when in bloom. Otherwise, use a tripod of tall, stout stakes to support it at the back of a border, or grow it up an obelisk. On a wall or pillar is probably the tidiest option, if you don't mind restraining those arching stems.

CARE AND MAINTENANCE

This rose needs a little effort to keep it looking at its best. Give it granular plant food in spring, along with a mulch of well-rotted manure or garden compost; keeping the plant in healthy growth will reduce the risk of disease. Mildew can be an issue (see p.44), and in a bad year you may need to spray. Watch out for aphids—pick off any that appear. Remove faded blooms and tidy after flowering, deadheading and removing damaged or diseased wood. On established plants, one or two older stems can be removed at the base.

'William Lobb' has large, semi-double purple-pink flowers that appear in summer.

'CANARY BIRD'

If ever a rose was designed for lifting the spirits, 'Canary Bird' is it. Often the first rose of the season to flower, this large-growing shrub is one of the joys of the spring garden. Just as its soft fernlike foliage is starting to develop, it offers up multitudes of flat, single, sunshine-yellow flowers that open suddenly from pointed buds that line the plant's upright, then arching, spiny branches.

CULTIVAR NAME *Rosa xanthina* 'Canary Bird'
ROSE TYPE Group 3, Species rose
FLOWERING Just once a year, in spring
FLOWER SIZE Around 2 in (5 cm) across, held along stems
FLOWER SCENT Light, fruity perfume
VIGOR Strong
DISEASE RESISTANCE Excellent
HARDINESS –4°F (–20°C) or lower

The cheery blooms of 'Canary Bird' pair perfectly with golden daffodils.

FEATURES

The display of this glorious rose starts in early spring, with new growth emerging from thorny stems, complete with masses of slender, pointed buds. These develop quickly and the first five-petaled blooms soon appear, upward facing, wide and flat, and in a sunshine-yellow color. The flowers, which attract many pollinators, have a light, fruity scent. Fernlike leaves follow, and then, in the fall, occasional purple hips. The stems of this large plant are upright at first, then arching, and can reach 8 ft (2.5 m) in height.

GARDEN USES

This is an ideal rose for adding spring interest to a sunny border, but it also looks lovely planted on its own at the edge of a woodland area or as a specimen in an island bed. It is a large plant that grows best in dappled shade, thriving if allowed sufficient space to develop its natural form. It is stunning when underplanted with blue *Muscari*, and is a great contrast to the first flowering cherries. It is tough enough to tolerate a summer-flowering clematis scrambling up its stems to add interest later in the year. 'Canary Bird' may be grown as a weeping standard, which is great if you have limited space.

CARE AND MAINTENANCE

This plant could not be simpler to keep. In spring, give it granular fertilizer and manure mulch over the roots to keep them moist—it does not like to be too dry. It is rarely beset by disease or the traditional problems. If it suffers occasional die-back, cut out the affected branches and it will soon recover. Keep pruning to a minimum—if the plant gets ungainly, remove an individual stem at ground level to keep it within bounds.

Arching stems with spectacular cascading blooms enjoy having space to spread.

Rosa 'Seagull' is a Rambler capable of quickly covering small buildings: make sure to give it adequate space and sturdy support.

GROUP 4: CLIMBING ROSES AND RAMBLERS

Cover fences and walls and create decorative garden features with roses from this category. Climbers and Ramblers are perhaps the most useful of all roses, mingling easily with existing plants, forming cascades from trees and pergolas, or gracing arches or arbors. If you have a warm, sheltered wall you can enjoy some of the more tender Climbers, while the most vigorous Ramblers are able to cover and disguise an entire outbuilding.

'ALBERTINE'

'Albertine' is a distinctive and much-loved old Rambler. It is adored for its generous displays of glowing pink, double, somewhat loosely formed flowers that open from charming reddish buds. Strongly scented, these are produced on vigorous, thorny growth beside handsome, bronze-tinted, glossy foliage. This is a perfect rose for relaxed plantings, where it can be allowed to grow freely.

CULTIVAR NAME 'Albertine'
ROSE TYPE Group 4, Rambler
FLOWERING Just once a year, in early- to mid-summer
FLOWER SIZE Around 3½ in (9 cm) across, in small clusters
FLOWER SCENT Powerful fruity perfume
VIGOR Strong
DISEASE RESISTANCE Tolerable
HARDINESS −4°F (−20°C)

Striking coppery-pink blooms are one of the attractions of this popular rose.

FEATURES

Raised in France in 1921 by the Barbier nursery, 'Albertine' is popular for its romantic displays of soft pink flowers that appear in profusion in early to midsummer. The open flowers are loose petaled and fade to blush pink; their fruity scent is superb. Plants are vigorous, with glossy, bronze-tinged foliage; the stems are armed with hooked spines. Plants reach around 15 ft (5 m) tall and across. Reddish hips may form.

GARDEN USES

For best results, grow this rose in full sun, though it will stand an open north-facing site. It thrives in rich,

well-drained soil, and always needs plenty of space. The classic location for this rose is on a house wall, where the perfume from its generous flowers can be admired by all. However, 'Albertine' is not a repeat-flowering selection, so it makes sense to pair it with another climber, perhaps *Clematis viticella*, for a longer display. 'Albertine' also looks terrific on a large pergola, but it is ultimately too large for a small rose arch. If you are eager to grow it on a fence or trellis, bear in mind that you will need to use sturdy supports. It is a lovely flower for adding to a posy.

CARE AND MAINTENANCE

This rose is easy to keep. Give it granular plant food in spring along with a mulch of well-rotted manure. Disease issues can arise in summer, often after flowering—it is prone to mildew and blackspot (see p.44). If in an open site, the attacks can usually be tolerated, but in a bad year you may need to cut out affected growth or even spray with fungicide. Water well in drought to avoid stress and pick off any aphids should they appear. Prune as for other Group 4 roses (see p.40).

'Albertine' makes a stunning display around early to midsummer.

'ALISTER STELLA GRAY'

This excellent Rambler is one of few that reliably repeats its displays of flowers—in this case, delicate clusters of rosette-shaped, egg-yellow, well-scented blooms that gradually fade to cream. Its strong-growing, climbing stems have few thorns, making it a useful plant around the garden—training wayward shoots is a far less hazardous task than with some other roses.

CULTIVAR NAME 'Alister Stella Gray'
ROSE TYPE Group 4, Rambler
FLOWERING Early to midsummer and again in early fall
FLOWER SIZE 2–2¼ in (5–6 cm) across, held in clusters
FLOWER SCENT Tea-rose perfume
VIGOR Strong
DISEASE RESISTANCE Fair
HARDINESS 5°F (–15°C)

FEATURES

Dating from 1894 and raised in Scotland by Alexander Hill Gray, this splendid Rambler has much to recommend it. The flowers are a delight—fairly small, but attractively rosette-shaped and held in graceful, nodding clusters, and with a good tea-rose scent. They open egg-yolk yellow, then fade to cream.

The color of this rose is richest in the center of the flower.

This display is repeated late in the season, adding greatly to the plant's garden value. It is vigorous-growing, but not dauntingly so, reaching a height and diameter of around 13 ft (4 m).

GARDEN USES

Choose a wall, fence, or pergola for this rose, ideally in full sun; it will take some shade, but must have space to spread. Supporting wires or trellis should be sturdy enough to hold a mature plant in full growth. Position it on a boundary at the back of a border for a flower-filled backdrop to planting, or drape it over a large archway. It can also be trained onto a post and rope rose catenary. If you have lots of space, try it as a free-standing, arching shrub.

CARE AND MAINTENANCE

Vigorous, healthy-growing, and simple in its care needs, this Rambler responds well to granular plant food in spring and a mulch of well-rotted manure. Disease issues, especially with blackspot (see p.44), may arise in summer. If in an open, sunny site, attacks should be minor, but you may need to spray in a bad year, and water, if it gets too dry. Clear the area of debris and cut out affected growth. Watch for aphids and rub them off if they appear. Prune as for Group 4 roses (see p.40).

ALSO TRY

Ramblers with few thorns include:
- *R. banksiae var. banksiae* **'Lutea'** produces its cascades of double yellow flowers early in the season.
- *R.* **MALVERN HILLS** **('Auscanary')** is a fine modern Rambler, with clusters of musk-scented pale yellow/cream flowers; it repeats through summer.
- *R.* **'Veilchenblau'** (pictured above) has small semi-double, scented flowers of an unusual purple-blue hue.

LADY BANKS' ROSE

This early-flowering rambling rose is commonly known as Lady Banks' Rose. It produces masses of small, sunshine-yellow double flowers in late spring. It fares best when attached to a sheltered, sunny wall with plenty of space for growth, because it will develop into a large plant. The arching stems are bright green and the glossy foliage lasts almost year-round in a mild winter.

CULTIVAR NAME *Rosa banksiae* 'Lutea'

ROSE TYPE Group 4, Rambler

FLOWERING Just once a year in late spring/early summer

FLOWER SIZE Around 1 in (2.5 cm) across, held in large bunches

FLOWER SCENT Faint, said to be like that of violets

VIGOR Very strong; stems grow up to 10 ft (3 m) in a season

DISEASE RESISTANCE Good

HARDINESS 14°F (−10°C)

Generous, showy bunches of flowers decorate a late spring garden.

FEATURES

This vigorous rambling rose was introduced into Europe from China in the 1820s. It is a highlight of late spring, when its cascades of arching, thornless stems become covered with dense masses of yellow double flowers and its petals shower the ground with gold as they fall. The blooms have a light perfume, similar to that of violets.

Lady Banks' Rose is a large climber, capable of reaching a height of around 40 ft (12 m) and spreading up to 20 ft (6 m) across. The leaves have five leaflets and will remain on the plant in a mild winter; fresh foliage grows just after flowering. Old stems develop peeling, copper-colored bark. The plant's evergreen nature makes it popular with roosting birds, adding to its value in the garden.

GARDEN USES

Lady Banks' rose is ideal for training up a tall house wall, although it can also be grown over outbuildings or—in milder areas—through a large tree. The stems need to be securely attached to wires or on trellis; younger growth should be tied but allowed to arch outward to create impressive cascading displays. This is not a plant for formal use—for example on a pergola—because its vigor and size make it hard to control. Lady Banks' Rose suits a relaxed presentation and looks great alongside *Wisteria* and *Clematis montana*, both of which flourish in similar conditions.

CARE AND MAINTENANCE

This rose grows strongly against a sheltered, sunny wall that protects the plant from late frosts and allows wood to ripen. Controlling growth is the main challenge. Excessive summer growth should be cut back to prevent the rose from obstructing gutters—long-armed tree pruners are the ideal tool.

Lady Banks' Rose flowers on wood made the previous year. To promote the growth of vigorous new shoots, remove a third of stems near their bases after flowering. This rose does not need deadheading and gets few problems: plants recover from odd mildew attacks without treatment.

This rose needs a sturdy support and can be used to cover entire walls.

'CECILE BRUNNER'

This climber has long been popular for its pale pink double flowers. Though they are relatively small, they are sweetly scented and grow in profusion in sprays on reddish, almost thornless, stems through much of summer. The rose is usually trouble-free and grows well even on a lightly shaded wall; it makes a great choice for a large pergola and will even cover an unsightly outbuilding in time.

CULTIVAR NAME 'Cecile Brunner'
ROSE TYPE Group 4, climbing Polyantha
FLOWERING Just once a year in late spring/early summer
FLOWER SIZE 1½ in (4 cm) across, held in clusters
FLOWER SCENT Sweetly fragrant
VIGOR Strong
DISEASE RESISTANCE Good
HARDINESS Around 5°F (−15°C)

A profusion of small, pink-tinted flowers is typical of this rose.

FEATURES

This climber, sometimes known as sweetheart rose, was introduced at the end of the 19th century. It is a versatile plant that thrives in a range of situations and offers a wealth of double pink flowers in spring, with more again opening in early summer. Each scented flower is exquisite—small but petal-filled, and rich pink in the center, opening from an elegant pointed bud. The dark green foliage can be quite dense and shows off the clusters of flowers well, while the red-tinged stems have few thorns. It is a strong, tall climber little troubled by pests or diseases and can reach around 23 ft (7 m) high and 13 ft (4 m) across. The dense growth provides good shelter for birds and other wildlife.

GARDEN USES

High vigor and a tough constitution make 'Cecile Brunner' a versatile plant. It will thrive in quite poor soil and even on lightly shaded walls, and stands summer heat well once established. It does need a reasonable amount of space. The rose is ideal for covering a wall or an expanse of sturdy fence, but you can also train it to grow through trees and over outbuildings or a pergola. It becomes too large to suit planting on a rose arch but its generous growth perfectly matches a relaxed cottage garden. The individual flowers make great buttonholes and are attractive in small posies.

CARE AND MAINTENANCE

This climber is straightforward to grow but needs regular training and pruning to keep it within bounds. Ensure that its supports are sturdy and that wires and trellis are firmly attached to walls because the weight of growth can be considerable. 'Cecile Brunner' does not require deadheading but does need annual pruning. This should be undertaken in winter by removing the oldest third of stems at their base.

ALSO TRY

Other wall-cover roses include:
- **R. Strawberry Hill ('Ausrimini')** bears honey-scented clusters of pink flowers.
- **R. 'Alister Stella Gray'** has yellow flowers with deeply colored centers.
- **R. 'Phyllis Bide'** (pictured below) produces semi-double blooms over a long season.

'CLIMBING LADY HILLINGDON'

This garden aristocrat, introduced in 1917, is one of the most graceful and desirable of all climbing roses. Huge nodding, semi-double flowers, in a dreamy apricot-yellow, open from elegant pointed buds that are held on slender stems.

CULTIVAR NAME 'Climbing Lady Hillingdon'
ROSE TYPE Group 4, Climbing Tea rose
FLOWERING Repeats from late spring into fall
FLOWER SIZE Around 5½ in (14 cm) across, held singly or in small clusters
FLOWER SCENT Tea rose
VIGOR Average
DISEASE RESISTANCE Fair
HARDINESS 14°F (−10°C)

FEATURES

Few roses have as much old-fashioned grace as 'Climbing Lady Hillingdon'. Its growth is richly purple-tinged (both stems and young leaves) and from late spring it bears large, loosely petaled flowers. The blooms are a lovely, glowing tone of apricot-yellow and have great character, nodding from their slender stems. The flowers have a powerful musky Tea-rose scent and repeat well through the season, often looking impressive right up until the first frosts. The plant reaches around 10 ft (3 m) in height.

GARDEN USES

This climber needs a warm place in full sun, ideally with the shelter of a wall, especially a house wall. In milder districts, it should also be happy trained on a sheltered fence. Individual flowers look fabulous displayed indoors. This rose is striking if paired with a less

The stunning yellow blooms often grace the gardens of historic houses.

vigorous honeysuckle, such as the coral-flowered *Lonicera sempervirens* 'Dropmore Scarlet'.

CARE AND MAINTENANCE

Although quite tender, 'Climbing Lady Hillingdon' is not a difficult rose to care for if you can find a suitable spot for it (see *above*). For best results, however, it benefits from some attention. Apply a dose of granular plant food and a mulch of well-rotted manure in spring. Watch out for disease as soon as growth starts; though this rose is quite resistant, blackspot, mildew, and rust are all possible (see p.44). If any of these occur, remove affected foliage. Keep the rose clear of debris and check for aphids on new growth, rubbing them off as they appear. Prune as for other Group 4 roses (see p.40).

This rose is a terrific choice for a sunny but sheltered wall of a house.

'CONSTANCE SPRY'

This was the first of the English Roses from UK breeder David Austin. If you have space, this superb plant can be grown as a large arching shrub, but it is usually most effective when trained along a fence or on a wall. Its light pink, double flowers have a spicy myrrh scent and make a striking show in early summer. Deadheading after the individual blooms fade will produce the longest displays.

CULTIVAR NAME 'Constance Spry'
ROSE TYPE Group 4, Climber
FLOWERING Just once a year, in early summer
FLOWER SIZE Around 4in (10cm) across, in small clusters
FLOWER SCENT Powerful myrrh perfume
VIGOR Strong
DISEASE RESISTANCE Fair
HARDINESS Around −4°F (−20°C)

This **profuse-flowering rose** has gorgeous deeply cupped pink petals.

FEATURES

Introduced in 1961 by David Austin, this was the rose that began the long line of popular English roses. The selection still has many merits, making it a popular choice today. If you enjoy myrrh-scented roses, 'Constance Spry's' strong perfume is outstanding. The rounded, distinctively cupped flowers appear in a gorgeous shade of pink; the centers are richest in hue. A vigorous, leafy plant, its foliage is large and its stems notably thorny. The arching growth reaches around 16–20ft (5–6m) if trained up a support.

GARDEN USES

This is a particularly tall-growing Climber and one to consider if you have a significant area to cover, although it will need quite a bit of training and tying to its support. Happily, its thorny stems are tough and flexible so you can direct them horizontally along a wall or even a low picket fence. Alternatively, it looks great when trained up a freestanding tripod of wooden posts.

With its vigorous, leafy growth, this is the sort of rose that suits relaxed planting and less formal areas. However, it flowers only once a year, so you may want to allow late-flowering climbers such as *Clematis viticella* or *Lonicera periclymenum* 'Serotina' to scramble through its branches and boost garden appeal later in the summer. 'Constance Spry' will stand some shade.

CARE AND MAINTENANCE

This rose is simple to keep. Give it a dose of granular plant food in spring and a mulch of well-rotted manure after flowering. Diseases may appear after this—it is prone to mildew and rust (see *p.44*)—but grown well, attacks should be mild. Clear away any debris and remove old heads after flowering. You may need to spray with fungicide in a bad year and water in drought to avoid stress. Rub off aphids if they appear on new growth in spring. Prune as for Group 4 Climbers (see *p.40*).

ALSO TRY

Other climbing English roses include:
- **R. CLAIRE AUSTIN ('Ausprior')** (*pictured right*) is a beautiful rose with cream-white blooms that have great disease resistance and a strong myrrh-like fragrance.
- **R. MARY DELANY ('Ausorts')** has small pink flowers that open from delicately pointed buds in late spring. The loosely double flowers are borne in clusters on bronze-tinted shoots.

DIZZY HEIGHTS

Clusters of these beautifully formed, glowing red flowers repeat abundantly through the season until the first frosts. This, combined with a compact yet strong and impressively healthy constitution, makes DIZZY HEIGHTS an outstanding garden rose. It is a great choice for injecting a touch of romance into your plantings and will always impress when trained on a fence or grown over an arch.

CULTIVAR NAME 'Fryblissful'
ROSE TYPE Group 4, Climber
FLOWERING Repeats through summer and into fall
FLOWER SIZE Around 4¾ in (12 cm) across, in small clusters
FLOWER SCENT Light perfume
VIGOR Average
DISEASE RESISTANCE Excellent
HARDINESS Around −4°F (−20°C)

The glowing red blooms of DIZZY HEIGHTS stand out from glossy foliage.

FEATURES

This modern Climber was introduced by the UK-based Fryers Roses in 1999 and has plenty to recommend it. The plant's luscious, bright scarlet-red flowers are nothing short of stunning—large, fully double, and with a magnificent swirled petal arrangement on opening. They have a mild, fresh fragrance. Although a strong and sturdy plant, DIZZY HEIGHTS does not get unmanageably large, reaching around 10 ft (3 m) tall.

GARDEN USES

This is a versatile rose that is useful for a range of situations. You can plant it in the traditional way, trained up a house wall over the front door, where the continuing display of flowers means there will usually be a bloom to greet visitors in the growing season. It is also perfect for training on fence panels as it does not get too bulky. Alternatively, train it over an arch to make a romantic feature, grow it on a freestanding obelisk or tripod, or train around a pillar or post.

CARE AND MAINTENANCE

DIZZY HEIGHTS is straightforward to maintain and keep looking great. A granular plant food along with a mulch of well-rotted manure in spring should satisfy it through the year.

This is a rose with a cast-iron constitution that has been bred with excellent disease resistance, so you should never need to worry about blackspot, rust, or mildew. Keeping plants healthy and clean should be enough to prevent disease from taking hold. However, watch out for aphids on new growth in spring, and rub off any as they appear. This compact grower is simple to deadhead, which will result in reliable reflowering. Prune as for other Group 4 roses (see p.40).

'FÉLICITÉ-PERPÉTUE'

This antique Rambler has a gloriously musky perfume and is much-admired for its impressive garden performance, whether it is grown on a fence, a wall, a freestanding tripod, or even up a tree. Quite late in the season, it produces masses of small, cupped, fully double flowers of the palest pink—these are offset beautifully by the plant's dark green, glossy foliage.

CULTIVAR NAME 'Félicité-Perpétue'
ROSE TYPE Group 4, Rambler
FLOWERING Just once a year, in early to midsummer
FLOWER SIZE Around 1½in (4cm) across, in large clusters
FLOWER SCENT Musk perfume
VIGOR Strong
DISEASE RESISTANCE Fair
HARDINESS Around 5°F (−15°C)

Flowers open in the palest pink, then gradually fade to white.

FEATURES

Raised in France in around 1827, this marvelous old Rambler is popular today for its displays of pompom-like flowers that, on mature plants, develop in their hundreds. The blooms are held in cascading sprays from vigorous yet lightly thorned branches. The strongly musk-scented flowers open around midsummer from pink-tinted buds. The leaves are attractive, too—glossy, dark green, and, in a mild year, almost evergreen. This plant easily reaches 20ft (6m) or more in height and spread. Orange hips may appear in the fall.

GARDEN USES

'Félicité-Perpétue' needs space to thrive, but tolerates a range of conditions, including shade and poor soil. It looks great tumbling from a north-facing wall or clambering from a pergola, its flowers cascading from above. Train it up a large tripod or even direct it into a nearby tree. If you have an eyesore to cover, this may be the rose for you. It will soon overpower small rose arches.

CARE AND MAINTENANCE

Vigorous and easy, 'Félicité-Perpétue' needs remarkably little ongoing care once it has established. Disease problems may appear in summer—it is prone to powdery mildew in wet weather, so watch for any attacks (see p.44). Blackspot and rust can also affect this rose, although the plant's vigor usually makes any attacks tolerable. Keep the area clear of any fallen debris and have a good annual clear-up around the plant. This rose needs little pruning, unless it is spreading out of bounds—in which case, prune as for Group 4 Ramblers (see p.40).

This vigorous rose needs plenty of space to display its fabulous cascading blooms.

'GARDENERS' GLORY'

This Climber is widely regarded to be one of the most reliable of all roses. Throughout summer and into the fall, it freely produces sweetly scented large, double flowers in sunshine-yellow; initially, these are high-centered, but become cupped in form. With its remarkable disease resistance, 'Gardeners' Glory' performs exceptionally in places where most other roses struggle.

CULTIVAR NAME 'Gardeners' Glory'
ROSE TYPE Group 4, Climber
FLOWERING Repeats through summer and into fall
FLOWER SIZE Around 4¾ in (12 cm) across, in small clusters
FLOWER SCENT Strong, sweet perfume
VIGOR Average
DISEASE RESISTANCE Excellent
HARDINESS Around −4°F (−20°C)

FEATURES

A tour-de-force from UK rose breeder Christopher Warner, 'Gardeners' Glory' was introduced in 2007 and has become a favorite in modern gardens, chiefly for its bulletproof constitution. Its foliage is rich-green and superbly glossy, while the large, glowing yellow flowers are produced in small clusters throughout the growing season. Deliciously fragrant, they open with a shapely form and then gradually age to a more open, cupped flower. It is strong and sturdy but never too vigorous, reaching around 10 ft (3 m) in height, which makes it an ideal climbing rose for many gardens, and a great choice for first-time rose-growers.

GARDEN USES

'Gardeners' Glory' performs well in any aspect, even tolerating some shade and quite dry, rooty soil when established. This rose checks all the boxes. Train it on any fence or wall and it will thrive; it looks great at the back of a border and will tolerate mixed planting in front. It is not too strong-growing to train around a front door or to decorate an arch or small pergola. This is also a rose to consider for a freestanding obelisk or tripod. In wilder parts of the garden—as long as it is not in full shade all day—it will stand on its own, scrambling through small trees or large shrubs, its flowering stems cascading with color in summer.

CARE AND MAINTENANCE

'Gardeners' Glory' is one of the easiest of climbing roses to grow and usually needs very little attention once it is well-established. For best results, give it granular plant food and a mulch of well-rotted manure in spring. It is also advisable to deadhead the plant to encourage reflowering through the season. Even in less-than-ideal conditions, this rose is highly unlikely to suffer from disease, but if you do spot any trouble, simply remove the affected foliage. Prune as for other Group 4 Climbers (see p.40).

This sensational bright yellow rose is considered one of the finest of all climbers.

'MADAME ALFRED CARRIÈRE'

This easily grown old Climber has an exceptionally long flowering season. Blush, then white, loosely double flowers nod gracefully from its stems, singly or in small clusters. It is a tough rose, and one of the best choices for a north-facing wall.

CULTIVAR NAME 'Madame Alfred Carrière'
ROSE TYPE Group 4, Noisette
FLOWERING Repeats through summer and into fall
FLOWER SIZE 4 in (10 cm) across, singly or in clusters
FLOWER SCENT Sweet scent
VIGOR Strong
DISEASE RESISTANCE Excellent
HARDINESS 5°F (−15°C)

FEATURES

This antique climbing Noisette rose, raised in France in 1879 by Joseph Schwartz, remains a superlative choice. The double flowers open to a wonderful glowing blush-white, a hint of pink suffusing the nodding blooms. Flowers fade to almost pure white and have a pleasant sweet scent. Flowering starts in late spring and continues through the season in flushes until the first frosts. This vigorous plant grows to around 16 ft (5 m), with almost thorn-free branches and dark, glossy foliage that is more or less evergreen.

Tough and adaptable, this rose offers old-rose charm, but without the hassle.

GARDEN USES

This rose needs plenty of space to grow and is not suitable for smaller arches and fences, which it will quickly overpower. Instead, train it on a large fence or wall; if you have a north-facing site and like a big climbing rose, this is the one for you. 'Madame Alfred Carrière' will grow through small trees, or can be trained across a large pergola and will happily host another climber, such as a clematis, honeysuckle, or passion flower. It seems to revel in shade and tolerates underplanting well.

CARE AND MAINTENANCE

This is a sturdy, versatile rose. Once established, the main job is bending the stems to tie them in to wires, and annual pruning to remove old growth. For best displays, mulch around the plant in spring and add fertilizer, but this rose will perform well without such care. It is seldom troubled by disease; blackspot may appear, but it is usually light and easily ignored. Prune as for Group 4 Noisette roses (see p.40).

ALSO TRY

Roses for north-facing walls include:
- *R. CRÈME DE LA CRÈME ('Gancre')* (pictured above) has sweetly scented cream-colored flowers with yellow centers.
- *R. 'Maigold'* produces early, semi-double flowers of orange-yellow with musk perfume. It is a strong grower with good disease resistance.
- *R. SUMMER WINE ('Korizont')* is a tough rose with single or semi-double scented flowers of orange-pink fading to coral.

'NEW DAWN'

Introduced in 1930 from the US, 'New Dawn' is one of the most popular climbing roses in the world, thanks to its excellent repeat-flowering habit—the plant is wreathed in blooms for much of the summer and fall. The sweetly perfumed, semi-double flowers open from fat buds; soft pink in color, and richer in hue at the heart, they are held against dark, glossy leaves.

CULTIVAR NAME 'New Dawn'
ROSE TYPE Group 4, Climber
FLOWERING Repeats through summer and into fall
FLOWER SIZE Around 3 in (8 cm) across, held in clusters
FLOWER SCENT Sweet, apple-like perfume
VIGOR Average
DISEASE RESISTANCE Tolerable
HARDINESS Around −4°F (−20°C)

The soft pink blooms of 'New Dawn' are slightly richer in color at the center.

FEATURES

'New Dawn' is considered to be one of the first modern repeat-flowering Climbers. Its soft, silvery pink flowers open from rounded buds within large sprays. The blooms are initially high-centered, then cupped, and have a pleasant sweet fragrance; the foliage is dark and glossy, with fairly strong, but not excessive, growth. The plant reaches around 13 ft (4 m) high.

GARDEN USES

This rose is well-suited to both cottage gardens and modern gardens—it does not get too rampant and is great for training on wires or trellises attached to walls and fences. It tolerates partially

Give this climber a bit of space and it will reward you with flowers for months.

shaded north-facing sites well. It is suitable for a large arch and is a good choice for a pergola, pillar, or tripod, where its flowers can cascade down. 'New Dawn' needs some room to grow.

CARE AND MAINTENANCE

Generally reliable, 'New Dawn' is best when given a little attention. Use granular plant food in spring and apply a mulch of well-rotted manure to keep it healthy and flowering through the season. Disease problems appear in summer, usually after flowering—it is prone to mildew, rust, and blackspot, (see p.44) but if grown in an open site, attacks should be mild and manageable. Water during a drought and keep the area clear of debris. Rub off aphids on new growth as they appear. Prune as for Group 4 Climbers (see p.40).

OPEN ARMS

Among the most adaptable of all Ramblers, this selection is ideal for smaller modern gardens. It bears huge trusses of small, soft pink blooms that look fabulous on pergolas, obelisks, and tripods. OPEN ARMS has a long flowering season, is relatively compact, offers great disease resistance, and its open flowers with their prominent stamens will attract pollinators.

CULTIVAR NAME 'Chewpixel'
ROSE TYPE Group 4, Rambler
FLOWERING Repeats through summer and into fall
FLOWER SIZE Around 2 in (5 cm) across, held in large clusters
FLOWER SCENT Light musk perfume
VIGOR Strong growing
DISEASE RESISTANCE Excellent
HARDINESS Around −4°F (−20°C)

OPEN ARMS is quite compact, is easy to manage, and has great disease resistance.

FEATURES

Introduced in 1995, this is an excellent selection from UK breeder Christopher Warner. The charming semi-double flowers open in a soft coral-pink, paling with age. Open-centered, they have a mass of golden stamens and are held in outstandingly impressive cascading trusses for a showy display that—unusually for a rambling rose—repeats through the season. The foliage is dark green and glossy; the red-tinged stems reach just 10 ft (3 m) high.

GARDEN USES

Many rambling roses are large-growing, vigorous plants that will quickly dwarf a smaller space. OPEN ARMS, however, is a different proposition and has various uses in the garden. This is a miniature Rambler that you can happily grow over a small arch or train on wooden fence-panels, allowing its flowering stems to tumble gracefully down. It is a particularly good choice for growing up a pillar or onto a pergola, or as a plant for an obelisk or tripod; it will not overpower these free-standing structures. It also makes a sociable host for a not-too-vigorous clematis or honeysuckle. It is happy in all soil types and in all aspects, and will stand some shade in the garden.

CARE AND MAINTENANCE

This is the perfect rose for a new gardener. Once established, it needs little attention to perform brilliantly, apart from training and tying in. Give it granular plant food and a mulch of well-rotted manure around the base in spring. It is a compact-growing rambler, so you can reach faded flower heads to deadhead in order to get the best repeat displays. OPEN ARMS is unlikely to suffer diseases—if any are seen, remove affected foliage. Prune as for all Group 4 Ramblers (see p.40).

This lovely rambling rose has a yellow flush at the heart of each bloom.

'SEAGULL'

This impressive Rambler produces small single and semi-double white flowers, held in large clusters, in early summer. Each bloom has a gorgeous central boss of showy golden stamens. At its peak, 'Seagull' is smothered in masses of these superb blooms. This is a vigorous plant that needs space to thrive, but it tolerates a lightly shaded spot and is great for pollinators.

CULTIVAR NAME 'Seagull'
ROSE TYPE Group 4, Rambler
FLOWERING Just once a year, in summer
FLOWER SIZE 1¼–1½in (3–4cm) across, held in huge clusters
FLOWER SCENT Musk perfume
VIGOR Strong
DISEASE RESISTANCE Tolerable
HARDINESS Around −4°F (−20°C)

The small blooms, with their stunning golden stamens, are held in large clusters.

FEATURES

This spectacular Rambler, introduced in 1907, produces small blooms that appear in their thousands on mature plants. They are upward-facing, pure white, and single or semi-double, with a wonderful central tuft of golden stamens. 'Seagull' flowers just once a year, but its blooms are followed by displays of orange-red hips in the fall.

GARDEN USES

This is one of the best Ramblers for growing up a tree. Plant it a little way out from the trunk, train it into the canopy, and it will soon provide floral flourishes. Be sure to select a sturdy host as it will overpower smaller, slower species. You can also grow 'Seagull' on a large pergola or a north-facing wall, although it will be slightly less vigorous in shade than in sun. Train it on supporting wires or trellis, but make sure they can take the weight of a mature plant. It is too vigorous for an arch, tripod, or rose catenary.

CARE AND MAINTENANCE

'Seagull' needs little care once established. Disease, particularly blackspot (see p.44), may arise in summer, usually after flowering, but the plant's vigor makes attacks tolerable. After a wet, warm spring mildew may strike, but plants in sunny, open places should escape. Keep the area clear of any fallen debris and have a good annual clear-up around the plant. There is no need to deadhead as you will want to enjoy the hips, and retaining the faded heads will ensure this happens. Minimum pruning is required, unless the plant is spreading out of bounds, in which case, treat it as other Group 4 Ramblers (see p.40).

ALSO TRY

Other roses for scrambling through trees include:
- *R.* **'The Garland'** has well-scented blush-white semi-double flowers held in generous clusters. This is a good rose for pollinators.
- *R.* **'Kew Rambler'** (pictured below) is musk scented, with white-eyed pink flowers held in big trusses. It has good hips in fall and is great for pollinators.
- *R.* **'Rambling Rector'** has musk-scented white blooms in huge heads. It is tall-growing and good for pollinators.

STARLIGHT SYMPHONY

If you are looking for an easy-to-grow, relatively compact, disease-resistant rose that provides masses of natural-looking flowers, STARLIGHT SYMPHONY is a terrific choice. This beautiful repeat-flowering Climber grows in a range of sites and aspects, is suitable for training on a garden fence or over an arch, and great for attracting a wealth of insect pollinators to your garden.

CULTIVAR NAME 'Harwisdom'
ROSE TYPE Group 4, Climber
FLOWERING Repeats through summer
FLOWER SIZE 3–4 in (8–10 cm) across, held in clusters
FLOWER SCENT Light, sweet perfume
VIGOR Average
DISEASE RESISTANCE Excellent
HARDINESS Around 5°F (–15°C)

STARLIGHT SYMPHONY's blooms look almost like those of wild roses.

FEATURES

This distinctive modern Climber was introduced by Harkness Roses and named Rose of the Year in 2019 by the British Association of Rose Breeders. The pure white semi-double blooms are held in generous clusters. Each one is open-faced, slightly loose-petaled, and displays wonderful golden, red-flushed stamens. It has a long, generous flowering habit that lasts all summer. The foliage of STARLIGHT SYMPHONY is glossy and apple green, and, although strong-growing, plants seem to stay fairly compact, reaching a height of around 10 ft (3 m).

GARDEN USES

STARLIGHT SYMPHONY fits well into modern gardens. Its unfussy flowers look great in an informal setting and while strong, the plant never gets too big, so it won't overpower a wooden fence, small rose arch, or pergola. Train it around an arch or doorway, plant it up a tripod, or use it with less vigorous climbers—perhaps purple, summer-flowering Clematis 'Ville de Lyon' or 'Perle d'Azur' for a touch of floral contrast. It certainly likes sun best, but will grow on a north-facing fence, as long as it is not too shaded.

CARE AND MAINTENANCE

This rose is easy to keep looking great, thanks to its disease resistance and its naturally compact habit. Train and tie the shoots in to wires and deadhead any faded blooms that you can easily reach to promote reflowering through summer. Keep an eye out for aphids and rub off any you see. Tidy and mulch around the base of the plant in spring and add granular fertilizer and a compost mulch to ensure the best performance. Prune as for all Group 4 Climbers (see p.40).

Rosa banksiae **'Lutea'** is a semi-evergreen Rambler that, given space, works well in cottage-style gardens and as a screen for outbuildings.

SUMMER WINE

Appealing and highly distinctive, this rose produces simple flowers that are a glowing orange-pink with near-yellow centers when they open, and then age to a rich coral-pink. With deadheading, these gorgeous blooms will appear in flushes throughout the summer. They are sometimes followed by an additional bonus—impressive displays of red hips, which last until late winter.

CULTIVAR NAME 'Korizont'
ROSE TYPE Group 4, Climber
FLOWERING Repeats through summer and into fall
FLOWER SIZE Around 4 in (10 cm) across, singly or in small clusters
FLOWER SCENT Sweet perfume
VIGOR Average
DISEASE RESISTANCE Good
HARDINESS Around −4°F (−20°C)

The simple blooms of SUMMER WINE have a striking two-tone appearance.

FEATURES

Developed by German rose breeders Kordes and introduced in 1984, SUMMER WINE is a Climber that has open single (or semi-double) flowers. They are held in clusters and emerge from orange buds. The petals, initially glowing orange-pink, age to a delightful coral color, while the centers are yellow with red stamens; this makes the clusters impressively colorful when they contain blooms of different ages. The flowers are strongly scented and attractive to pollinators. They are offset by dark green, glossy foliage.

ALSO TRY

Other simple-flowered climbers are:
- *R.* ALTISSIMO (**'Delmur'**) has large, single, rich-red blooms and repeats through summer.
  R. **'Mermaid'** is a strong-growing rose with single, pale yellow blooms, each with a glowing heart. It repeats well and has some scent.
- *R.* THE SIMPLE LIFE (**'Hartrifle'**) (pictured right) has charming single peach-pink flowers that are repeated through summer. It has some scent and is not too vigorous.

At the end of the year, bunches of showy, fat, red hips may develop. This is a sturdy, quite thorny plant that grows to 13 ft (4 m) in height.

GARDEN USES

An easy and vigorous climber, SUMMER WINE is also highly versatile. It is not picky about soil or location and can be used in a variety of ways. With its good tolerance of shade, it can be grown along a fence or wall—even one that faces north—producing a dense display of color through the summer and fall. Try this rose at the back of a mixed border—it doesn't mind a little competition—or grown through a small

tree. With its simple flowers and sweet scent, it helps create a relaxing atmosphere in your garden.

CARE AND MAINTENANCE

This rose is usually hassle free. Training and bending the plant to tie it in to wires can be a challenge because the stems are quite thorny and get quite stout. For the best displays, mulch around the base of the plant in spring and add fertilizer. It is seldom troubled by diseases—blackspot, rust, and mildew may strike, but are rarely anything to worry about, as long as you maintain good garden hygiene. Prune as for other Group 4 Climbers (see p.40).

THE GENEROUS GARDENER

This is an easily grown modern Climber that provides plenty of old-rose appeal. It produces masses of soft pink, rounded, double flowers that open in small, nodding clusters. A strong, vigorous rose, THE GENEROUS GARDENER is highly disease resistant, repeats well, and is a great choice for a north-facing wall. The scent—a powerful old-fashioned rose perfume—is another outstanding feature of this selection.

CULTIVAR NAME 'Ausdrawn'
ROSE TYPE Group 4, Climber
FLOWERING Repeats through summer and into fall
FLOWER SIZE 2¼–2¾ in (6–7 cm) across, in clusters
FLOWER SCENT Powerful old-rose perfume
VIGOR Strong growing
DISEASE RESISTANCE Excellent
HARDINESS −4°F (−20°C)

FEATURES

Introduced in 2002 by UK breeder David Austin, this exquisite cultivar has much to offer, as its name suggests. The rosette-shaped, soft pink blooms are not the largest, but they are beautifully formed, opening from pointed, rich pink buds. Large clusters of the flowers nod gracefully from the plant and often attract bees. The scent has a rich myrrh-like quality and the mid-green foliage is the perfect foil to those lovely blooms. If the plant is not deadheaded, showy orange-red hips may form at the end of the season. Growth is strong, to 13–16 ft (4–5 m).

The exquisite blooms are cupped, rounded, and open-hearted.

GARDEN USES

This plant should be near the top of your list if you need an eye-catching Climber. Although it can reach a large size, it can be kept within bounds by judicious pruning and training. You can grow this rose on a large, strong fence, on a wall, even up the front of a house; it is robust enough to do well on a north-facing site. It can be trained over a pergola; through a small tree; or on a large, sturdy archway. With its relaxed habit, THE GENEROUS GARDENER looks great in a cottage garden or more traditional setting, and its glorious scent makes it a strong candidate for cutting and bringing indoors.

CARE AND MAINTENANCE

This plant is relatively simple to grow, making it an ideal choice for those who want the old-rose look without too much work. The main job is training and tying in its shoots, which are stout and strong-growing.

Give the plant a decent mulch of manure or garden compost in spring and add granular fertilizer to ensure the best floral displays. Deadhead any faded trusses you can reach. THE GENEROUS GARDENER is seldom troubled by disease, except in particularly hot or very wet summers. Prune as for Group 4 Climbers (see p.40).

ALSO TRY

Other impressive scented Climbers include:
- *R. 'Climbing Blue Moon'* has huge, shapely, silvery-mauve flowers, held singly or in clusters, in flushes throughout the summer. The blooms have a powerful, fruity perfume.
- *R. SCENT FROM HEAVEN* **('Chewbabaluv')** (pictured below) was Rose of the Year 2017. It has shapely orange flowers all summer; a powerful, fruity scent; and excellent disease resistance.

THE PILGRIM

Probably the best known Climber from UK breeder David Austin, THE PILGRIM features glorious, fully double rosette-shaped sulfur-yellow flowers. The color is richest in the center of each bloom and fades to cream around its edges. The rose flowers generously, even from the base of the plant, which makes it extremely useful in the garden, especially for growing up walls and pillars.

CULTIVAR NAME 'Auswalker'
ROSE TYPE Group 4, Climber
FLOWERING Repeats through summer and into fall
FLOWER SIZE Around 4¾in (12cm) across, usually in small clusters
FLOWER SCENT Tea-rose perfume
VIGOR Average
DISEASE RESISTANCE Good
HARDINESS −4°F (−20°C)

Stunning soft yellow blooms are among the many attractions of this rose.

FEATURES

The beautifully formed flowers of THE PILGRIM are irresistible to many gardeners, which is why this fine Climber has found a home in numerous gardens since its introduction in 1991. A wealth of useful attributes puts it ahead of its competitors. The first impressive and generous flush of the well-scented, large, rosette-shaped yellow flowers appears in early summer. If you deadhead the flowers, more clusters of magnificent blooms will readily follow. THE PILGRIM flowers well low down on the plant, providing a wall of color from almost the ground up to a height of about 10ft (3m), making it perfect for growing up walls where full, dense coverage is required.

GARDEN USES

This plant is a great all-rounder. It is perfect grown simply on wires or trellis attached to a fence or wall, even at a north-facing site or a relatively shady spot. Growth is strong and healthy but not overpowering. THE PILGRIM also makes a lovely choice for a rose arch, tripod, rose catenary, or obelisk because it looks good from afar, with the lower parts of the plant well-furnished with foliage and flowers. It is also a welcome sight cascading from a pergola or even above a front door.

CARE AND MAINTENANCE

This rose is quite easy to care for. Apply granular plant food in spring along with a mulch of well-rotted manure or garden compost to keep it doing well all season. Remove debris from around the plant and clear away fallen petals. Deadhead as well as you can after flowering—this will help keep disease at bay, though THE PILGRIM is a fairly resistant selection. Watch out for aphids on new growth in spring and rub them off as they appear. Prune as for Group 4 Climbers (see p.40).

This versatile rose has good disease resistance and stands shade well.

WARM WELCOME

This dazzling rose from UK rose breeder Christopher Warner stands out both for its glowing orange blooms—produced in multitudes throughout summer and into the fall—and for its diminutive stature. This is a climbing Miniature rose, and is ideally suited to small modern gardens. Easy to grow and with good disease resistance, this charming little plant has plenty going for it.

CULTIVAR NAME 'Chewizz'
ROSE TYPE Group 4, Climber
FLOWERING Repeats through summer and into fall
FLOWER SIZE Around 2 in (5 cm) across, held in clusters
FLOWER SCENT Light
VIGOR Average
DISEASE RESISTANCE Good
HARDINESS Around −4°F (−20°C)

Bright, deep orange blooms sing out from glossy green foliage.

FEATURES

Introduced by UK breeder Christopher Warner in 1987, Warm Welcome is a fabulous Climber for smaller spaces. Its flowers are semi-double, developing from reddish buds and becoming fully open-faced when mature. The glorious blooms are a glowing shade of orange, which is made all the more impressive when contrasted with the plant's dark, somewhat dainty, glossy foliage. The flowers have a light, sweet perfume and are held in generous, upright trusses, appearing freely throughout summer and into the fall. An added bonus is that Warm Welcome holds on well to its lower growth, flowering even toward the base of the plant. It reaches around 8 ft (2.5 m) in height.

GARDEN USES

As its name suggests, Warm Welcome is the perfect selection for growing up a wall and above the front door. Its slender, easily trained growth stays neat, and flowers from low down to form an impressive expanse of blooms. The plant grows well on a small rose arch, up through an obelisk, or trained around a pillar or post; it will never overpower the structure. You can easily keep it within bounds on a sunny fence, and it can grow well in a large container, something few other climbers will tolerate for long. It likes a sunny spot and grows best on its own, so is well-suited to small spaces.

CARE AND MAINTENANCE

Warm Welcome is a fairly hassle-free rose. Give it granular fertilizer and a compost mulch in spring to promote great displays through the summer. Be sure to deadhead regularly so flowers repeat. In hot weather, give it a little water to help maintain good health. It is resistant to problems, but blackspot and mildew are possible (see p.44); the plant is compact, so affected growth can be easily removed. If you are growing this plant in a container, provide plenty of water and feed in summer. This rose needs only a light prune in winter (see p.40).

ALSO TRY

Other miniature Climbers include:
- **R. Purple Skyliner ('Franwekpurp')** has pale green foliage and scented purple flowers that age to mauve.
- **R. 'Star Performer'** (pictured below) is lightly scented, with pink flowers in clusters and shiny rich green foliage.
- **R. White Star ('Harquill')** has scented white, semi-double flowers and is strong growing.

With its dense, bushy growth; easygoing character; and glorious displays of delicate pink flowers all summer long, *Rosa* BONICA has found a home in many modern gardens.

GROUP 5: GROUND COVER ROSES

Members of this group are among the most versatile of all roses. Many will grow in part shade and need very little in the way of annual pruning. They may have an impressively long flowering season, repeating well and providing carpets of color in the garden. Tumble them down a bank, grow them below high tree canopies, use them in an island bed, or plant them in a large container and let the stems spill appealingly over the edges.

BONICA

This rose has a tough, easy-going constitution, which it backs up with a nonstop display of semi-double pink flowers held in sprays from late June. It repeats well into the fall, after which decorative orange hips may form. With neat, rather bushy growth, it suffers few problems, thriving in sun or part-shade and offering reliable cover in a variety of locations.

CULTIVAR NAME 'Meidomonac'
ROSE TYPE Group 5, Ground Cover
FLOWERING Repeats through summer and into fall
FLOWER SIZE 2⅓ in (6 cm) across, held in clusters
FLOWER SCENT Light perfume
VIGOR Average
DISEASE RESISTANCE Excellent
HARDINESS Around −4°F (−20°C)

Vigorous BONICA will grow happily in partial shade.

Flower color is richest at the heart of each semi-double bloom.

FEATURES

Although BONICA is classed as a Ground Cover selection, it is a rather shrubby plant, reaching around 3 ft (1 m) or more in height. It does not produce low, ground-hugging growth and yet is suitable for massed planting, forming dense twiggy plants with glossy, dark green foliage. Its dainty pink flowers are held in large sprays of around nine or more flowers atop tall stems. The first long-lasting flush of flower begins in early summer and repeats into fall.

GARDEN USES

BONICA grows well in sun and part shade, even surviving below tree canopies, and tolerates any aspect and soil, as long as it is well drained. When planted en masse, the shrubs knit together, filling borders with color and forming what is essentially high-level ground cover. It is suitable for planting on slopes, where its flowers cascade down elegantly, and is at home in cottage-style gardens as well as more modern and formal spaces. In mixed borders it is tough enough to withstand some competition and works well alongside plants such as catmint and lavender. It thrives in containers, too.

CARE AND MAINTENANCE

This plant needs next to no upkeep, making it one of the most useful of all garden roses. A spring feed of granular plant food and a mulch of well-rotted manure will keep it in healthy growth all year, but even if you forget, this rose will forgive you. Deadhead regularly for repeat flowering through summer, and clear away fallen petals and leaves from the base as these can harbor disease. Pruning needs are simple: remove dead or diseased wood or rubbing branches and then reduce stems by around a third to a half (see p.41).

CENTRE STAGE

This first-rate ground-covering rose was developed by UK breeder Christopher Warner and introduced in 2001. It has extremely low-growing stems that bear dainty foliage and masses of pale pink, usually five-petaled, lightly scented single flowers that smother the branches. It repeats reliably through the summer, attracting insect pollinators to the garden.

CULTIVAR NAME 'Chewcreepy'
ROSE TYPE Group 5, Ground Cover
FLOWERING Repeats through summer and into fall
FLOWER SIZE 1⅛ in (3 cm) across, held in clusters
FLOWER SCENT Light musky perfume
VIGOR Strong
DISEASE RESISTANCE Excellent
HARDINESS Around −4°F (−20°C)

FEATURES

Centre Stage makes a spectacular sight when grown in quantity, its small but wonderfully profuse flowers creating a carpet of color. It is a low-growing plant with creeping stems that are no more than 12 in (30 cm) tall. Over time, and after multiple prunings, its growth can take the form of a mound. Its leaves are small and dark, and the flowers have five well-spaced, pink petals that shiver around a golden crown of stamens, providing a distinctly musky scent. Although it is somewhat fragile in appearance, it is a tough customer that produces plenty of flowers all summer on a plant that could scarcely be simpler to grow.

GARDEN USES

With its low-growing habit, this rose is one of the best for cover, its stems slinking across the ground, weaving between other plants. Centre Stage prefers a sunny place but stands a little shade, and will work in almost any well-drained soil. It is perfect for growing down a bank, mound, or over a wall; it will even fill a large rock garden with color. You could use it in gravel gardens for low-level flower power and it makes a wonderful sight in a large container, its wreathed stems cascading down over the edges.

CARE AND MAINTENANCE

The key to growing Centre Stage successfully is to plant it where it has plenty of space to spread. Beyond this consideration, the plant is tough, resistant to disease, and needs little care. If you can get near its roots, spread a little granular plant food in spring: mulching is unlikely to be an option because of the dense growth. Deadhead wherever you can reach the flowers, but this is far from essential. Pruning is simple: cut back stems by a third where the plant threatens to outgrow its space (see p.41).

Individual plants can spread to a width of more than 3 ft (1 m).

FLOWER CARPET CORAL

Noack Rosen of Germany have bred an outstanding range of Ground Cover roses in many colors, and this 2001 selection is among the best. It blooms continuously from late spring into fall, producing drifts of flowers that often mask the plant's glossy green foliage. The flowers are a most unusual hue—delicate coral-pink with a paler eye—and the plant has proven to be disease-resistant and tough.

CULTIVAR NAME 'Norlesa'
ROSE TYPE Group 5, Ground Cover
FLOWERING Repeats through summer and into fall
FLOWER SIZE 3⅛ in (8 cm) across, held in clusters
FLOWER SCENT Little perfume
VIGOR Average
DISEASE RESISTANCE Excellent
HARDINESS Around −4°F (−20°C)

FEATURES

The distinctive blooms of this rose begin to open before the end of spring, developing from fat, pointed buds held in generous clusters above healthy, dark green, glossy foliage. The single flowers emerge in a coral color, but become pinker with age and develop a paler eye. They appear by the hundreds on mature plants, more or less continuously into fall; decorative hips will sometimes form, too. Healthy plants will reach around 28 in (70 cm); they have a spreading habit, forming dense, twiggy cover.

Easy maintenance and pretty flowers make this Ground Cover rose a winner.

GARDEN USES

This durable and easy-growing rose is versatile, with many uses around the garden. It likes a sunny spot best but will tolerate shade through the day and is not picky about soil, as long as it is well drained. Planting these roses en masse will provide excellent ground cover, and quickly fill a difficult-to-cultivate bank. FLOWER CARPET CORAL can be planted below trees with high, light canopies or to fill an island bed with flowers. Used singly it will inject its unusual color into a mixed border, tumble over a low wall, or add impact to a gravel garden. It is also a great choice for a large pot, its stems spilling over the edges of the container.

CARE AND MAINTENANCE

Like most other Ground Cover roses, this plant is easy, thriving with little attention and seldom suffering disease. In spring, fertilize with granular feed, and—if access is possible—spread well-rotted manure over the roots. Deadhead individual plants to keep them tidy and promote repeat flowering, but this is not essential. Pruning is simple and as for other Ground Cover roses (see p.41): remove dead or diseased wood or rubbing branches and then cut back stems with shears by around a third to a half.

ALSO TRY

Other Flower Carpet roses from Noack Rosen offer color variations:

- **_R._ FLOWER CARPET RED VELVET ('Noare')** (pictured above) has deep red single flowers with contrasting yellow stamens.
- **_R._ FLOWER CARPET SUNSHINE ('Noason')** has bunches of soft yellow semi-double flowers that fade to cream.
- **_R._ FLOWER CARPET WHITE ('Noaschnee')** is a terrific selection with pure white semi-double flowers that have sweet fragrance and stand out well from the rich foliage.

KENT

This rose was raised by Danish growers Olesen and sold from 1985 as part of the County Series Collection. It bears masses of cupped, white, semi-double flowers from early summer right through the growing season, so offers excellent decorative value. The plant has a low arching habit with healthy, glossy, dark foliage and stands poor soil and some shade well.

CULTIVAR NAME 'Poulcov'
ROSE TYPE Group 5, Ground Cover
FLOWERING Repeats through summer and into fall
FLOWER SIZE 1½in (4cm) across, held in clusters
FLOWER SCENT Little perfume
VIGOR Average
DISEASE RESISTANCE Good
HARDINESS Around −4°F (−20°C)

Neat, rounded bushes carry a profusion of white blooms.

FEATURES

Olesen's series of dainty Ground Cover roses is named for the counties of England. KENT has pretty, pure white flowers that are somewhat cupped when they first open but soon become flat, displaying golden stamens at their heart. They are held in generous trusses that contrast well with the dark green, glossy leaves. Growth is quite dense and reaches heights of around 24in (60cm) but at the same time the plant sends out spreading, arching stems that soon cover a large area and can be threaded between other shrubs, knitting together plantings. Disease resistance is good and this rose proves easy and useful to grow.

GARDEN USES

This super rose favors a sunny, well-drained site but will stand some shade. It is ideal for use in white-themed gardens because it produces blooms for such a long period and so can become the backbone of a planting plan. Use it singly or repeated toward the front of a border, where it will form mounds of flowers. Alternatively, grow KENT in a group and prune the plants into a low flowering hedge. This is another great rose for planting on a slope where the flowers will cascade down elegantly, or for elevating in a raised bed or large container. It is sometimes sold as a weeping standard.

CARE AND MAINTENANCE

This is another Ground Cover rose that thrives with minimal effort. Spread granular plant food in spring and try to fork well-rotted manure or garden compost around the roots, if possible. Tidy spent flowers and leaves through the season, deadheading the worst of the blooms. Pruning is easy (see p.41); remove any dead or diseased wood or rubbing branches; if the plant becomes too large, reduce stems by around a third to a half.

ALSO TRY

Other County Series roses from Olesen offer color variations:
- **R. HERTFORDSHIRE ('Kortenay')** has masses of vivid, single, red-pink flowers all summer on a healthy, low, bushy plant that is attractive to pollinators.
- **R. SURREY ('Korlanum')** (pictured right) has charming, semi-double, pollinator-friendly, soft pink flowers all summer. An excellent and healthy choice.

PARTRIDGE

This plant, introduced by German breeder Kordes in 1984, is among the toughest of Ground Cover roses. PARTRIDGE has charming, simple, white flowers, which are produced later in the season when other roses have begun to fade. Blooms open from pinkish buds that look like wild briar, and the rose has a similarly free-spirited habit. Its leafy, dense growth suppresses weeds and covers ground very well.

CULTIVAR NAME 'Korweirim'
ROSE TYPE Group 5, Ground Cover
FLOWERING Once, but over a long period in summer
FLOWER SIZE 1½ in (4 cm) across, held in clusters
FLOWER SCENT Strong musky perfume
VIGOR Strong
DISEASE RESISTANCE Excellent
HARDINESS Around 5°F (−15°C)

FEATURES

PARTRIDGE is a vigorous, almost rampant, plant that can reach a height of around 20 in (50 cm) when established, though it is usually lower. It can spread out several yards and is quite capable of rambling up walls and into trees given some support. The flowers start to open after many other roses have finished, usually in July. They are small, white, well-scented, and single, opening from pinkish buds held in trusses and have a rather wild look, freely attracting pollinators. Hips may form after the last blooms of the season. The thorny shoots are red-tinged when young and strong but slender with masses of glossy foliage that covers ground well, forming low mounds of growth.

GARDEN USES

This sturdy rose makes reliable low weed-suppressing ground cover. It prefers a sunny location but is happy in a little shade and on any soil as long as drainage is adequate. PARTRIDGE is the ideal choice if you want to disguise an ugly bank or cover an old tree stump. It does well below trees with high canopies, and will climb into them if given the chance. This is not a plant for limited spaces (or for containers) because it spreads and clambers wherever it can—making it perfect for wilder or tricky-to-cultivate parts of the garden.

CARE AND MAINTENANCE

Luckily for such a vigorous plant, PARTRIDGE seldom needs any attention. Just be sure to plant it where it will not outgrow its site. It is tough, easy, and disease resistant. Feeding and mulching are thankfully not needed because they are tricky once the plant is large, while deadheading is pointless as it only serves to prevent hips forming. Pruning is not needed; just shear back stems by around a third if the plant gets unruly.

This mound-forming rose produces clusters of white, single flowers.

SCENTED CARPET

Introduced in 2001 by UK breeder Christopher Warner, this is much more than a versatile Ground Cover plant. In summer and fall, it delights the senses with its masses of vibrant pink, white-centered flowers, which carry a heady, musky fragrance. A sea of pretty, five-petaled blooms is held above shining foliage, making this rose a great bet for borders, banks, and containers.

CULTIVAR NAME 'Chewground'
ROSE TYPE Group 5, Ground Cover
FLOWERING Repeats through summer and into fall
FLOWER SIZE 1½ in (4 cm) across, held in clusters
FLOWER SCENT Strong musky perfume
VIGOR Average
DISEASE RESISTANCE Excellent
HARDINESS Around −4°F (−20°C)

FEATURES

This rose freely produces flowers all summer and well into fall. They open from red-pink, pointed, clustered buds into vibrant cerise blooms with a distinctly contrasting white eye. With age, they fade to a softer tone of pink, giving the heads a two-tone appearance. SCENTED CARPET reaches heights of around 24 in (60 cm) and has a low, arching, spreading habit. Plants have small, shiny leaves, which offer excellent disease resistance. This rose is not too vigorous to use in a container or to plant in a smaller garden.

GARDEN USES

SCENTED CARPET loves a sunny site and will grow well on most well-drained soils. It is at its best where its arching stems are free to cascade: try it, for example, in a large container on the patio, where its long flowering and delicious scent can be enjoyed by all. Alternatively, try lifting a paving slab; improve the soil beneath and plant this rose so it can spill decoratively over the patio. It works well when planted next to a low wall where it can be trained to scramble over the top. You can also plant this rose toward the front of a sunny border, en-masse to fill an island bed with color, or in a gravel garden to add scent and vibrancy.

Unusually for a Ground Cover rose, this selection has an impressive scent.

CARE AND MAINTENANCE

This is an easy, disease-resistant rose that needs little ongoing care. Add a little granular plant food around its roots in spring and fork well-rotted manure or garden compost under the branches. Deadheading plants is possible if they are small or in a container, but not essential. Pruning is simple: cut back stems by around a third if the plant outgrows its space.

INDEX

Page numbers in **bold** refer to main entries.

Author Philip Clayton

AUTHOR ACKNOWLEDGMENTS
The author would like to thank Liam Beddall from David Austin Roses
and rose breeder Chris Warner for their help.

PUBLISHER ACKNOWLEDGMENTS
DK would like to thank Mary-Clare Jerram for developing the original concept;
Vanessa Bird for indexing; Diana Vowles for proofreading; and Paul Reid,
Marek Walisiewicz, and the Cobalt team for their hard work in putting this
book together.

PICTURE CREDITS
The publisher would like to thank the following for their kind permission
to reproduce their photographs:

Alamy Stock Photo: Alan Gregg 60bl; Alan Mather 82c; Alexandra Glen
58-59c, 139cr; Aliaksandr Mazurkevich 2c; Alice Musbach 20-21c;
amomentintime 75br; Andrei David 46cl; Anne Gilbert 94cl; Archival Survival
117bc, 53br, 114cl; Avalon.red 19c4, 23bl, 30bl, 34cr, 41bl, 47br, 71cr, 74cl, 108bl,
112br, 130cl; AY Images 97cl; BIOSPHOTO 76br, 110c, 119cl; blickwinkel 10-11c,
19b1, 39tr, 95cr; Bob Gibbons 8br; Botanic World 61br, 102bl, 109br, 134cl;
CHRIS BOSWORTH 17c, 105br, 121cr; Chris Lawrence 99cr; Chronicle 8bc;
Clare Gainey 44tr, 84cr; 100-101c, 119br, 129bl; Dave Bevan 45tc, 45bc;
Deborah Vernon 16bc, 18tc, 113bl; Denis Crawford 45tl; Dennis Frates 6c;
Derek Harris 135br; Dorling Kindersley ltd 49tr; Elena Cherkasova 13tr;
Elizabeth Whiting & Associates 27bc; Emmanuel LATTES 46br; Fir Mamat 49tl;
Floral Images 112cl; Garden Photo World 15tl, 19c2, 123cl, 130br; garfotos
14tr; GKSFlorapics 18tl; Glenn Harper 65cr; Gordon Scammell 56cl; Graham
Prentice 55cr, 81br; Graham Titchmarsh 81cl; Hervé Lenain 114br; Holmes
Garden Photos 26br, 41tr; JacHow 70cl; Jane Tregelles 14bl, 67cr, 122cl; John
Richmond 43cl, 43c; Jonathan Ward 19c3, 56cr, 66cl, 87br, 120bl, 131br, 132c;
Judith Bicking 73cr; Kevin Wheal 15bl, 77cr; Klaus Steinkamp 104c; Kumar
Sriskandan 22cr; Lesley Pardoe 106cl; Martin Hughes-Jones 99bl, 123br, 136bl;
Matthew Taylor 13cl, 14bc, 109cl; mauritius images GmbH 12bl; McPhoto/Rolf
Mueller 54cr; Michael Dutton 39br; Michael Hudson 8tr; Nigel Cattlin 44bc,
44br, 45bl; Ole Schoener 8bl; Olga Ionina 19b2; P Tomlins 72br, 88c, 124br;
Paul Maguire 34tr; PURPLE MARBLES GARDEN 27br; Radharc Images 34br;
Rex May 107cl; RM Floral 30tr,31cr, 50c, 63br; Roman Milert 33tr; Rosemary
Owen 97br; Sergey Kalyakin 27tr, 121bl; Sharon Talson 22tr; Steffen Hauser /
botanikfoto 27tc, 44bl; Steffie Shields 67bl; Steve Allen Travel Photography
34c; thrillerfillerspiller 54bl, 69cr; Tim Gainey 4c, 24c, 26bl, 27bl, 84bl, 116bl;
Trevor Chriss 93cr; Viktar Savanevch 34bc; Zoonar GmbH 9tc, 122cr.

Dorling Kindersley: Charles Quest-Ritson 62cr, 131cl; Chris Gibson 45br;
Dreamstime.com: Volodymyr Silichev/Vosilich18 12br; iStock: cjp 34cb; Mark
Winwood / Hampton Court Flower Show 2014 61cl; Mark Winwood / RHS
Wisley 16ca, 18br, 19b3, 52cl, 52br, 56bl, 62cl, 64bl, 64br, 68br, 76bl, 78-79c,
91cl, 92br, 115cl, 116cr; Peter Anderson 23br, 31tl, 47tr.

Dreamstime.com: Sarah2 47cl.

GAP Photos: 138bl; Andrea Jones 48cr, 48br; Dave Bevan 27tl; Friedrich
Strauss 32tr, 36-37c; Geoff du Feu 118cl; Howard Rice 49cl; Howard Rice -
Cambridge Botanic Gardens 103cr; Jacqui Dracup 125cl; John Glover 95bl;
Jonathan Buckley 35tr; Martin Hughes-Jones 80bl; Paul Debois 85cr; Richard
Wareham 129br.

Getty Images: Jaana Eleftheriou 46tr; Jacky Parker Photography 28-29c;
Photos from Japan, Asia and othe of the world 126-127c.

Getty Images / iStock: Andrew Linscott 86cl; Chamille White 9cl; Ellita
26tr; emer1940 104cl; joloei 42b; marinowifi 13bc; MSCTpics 48cl; Nattawat
Jindamaneesirikul 96bl; Nickbeer 12tr; Olga Evtushkova 49tc; Ruslan Dashinsky
9br; Serhii Ivashchuk 38cl; shuichi kadoya 14br; Supersmario 9cl.

Cover images: Front: GAP Photos: Howard Rice - David Austin Rose
Garden; Back: **Alamy Stock Photo:** Alexandra Glen tr, Clare Gainey cl

Illustrations by Debbie Maizels
All other images © Dorling Kindersley

Penguin Random House

Produced for DK by
COBALT ID
www.cobaltid.co.uk

Editors Marek Walisiewicz, Diana Loxley
Senior US Editor Megan Douglass
US Consultant John Tullock
Managing Art Editor Paul Reid
Art Editor Darren Bland

DK LONDON

Project Editor Lucy Philpott
Assistant Editor Jasmin Lennie
Senior Designer Glenda Fisher
Editorial Manager Ruth O'Rourke
Senior Production Editor Tony Phipps
Production Controller Kariss Ainsworth
Jacket Designer Nicola Powling
Jacket Co-ordinator Abi Gain
Art Director Maxine Pedliham
Publishing Director Katie Cowan

Consultant Gardening Publisher Chris Young

First American Edition, 2024
Published in the United States by DK Publishing
1745 Broadway, 20th Floor, New York, NY 10019

A catalog record for this book
is available from the Library of Congress.
ISBN: 978-0-7440-9229-5

Printed and bound in China

www.dk.com

MIX
Paper | Supporting
responsible forestry
FSC™ C018179

This book was made with Forest
Stewardship Council™ certified
paper—one small step in DK's
commitment to a sustainable future.
For more information, go to
www.dk.com/our-green-pledge.